KU-675-813

Your PhD Companion

Stephen Marshall and Nick Green

howtobooks

Published by
How To Books Ltd,
3 Newtec Place,
Magdalen Road,
Oxford OX4 1RE,
United Kingdom.
Tel: (01865) 793806   Fax: (01865) 248780
info@howtobooks.co.uk
www.howtobooks.co.uk

First edition 2004

British Library Cataloguing in Publication Data
A catalogue record for this book is available from the British Library

Produced for How To Books by Deer Park Productions, Tavistock
Typeset by Pantek Arts Ltd, Maidstone, Kent
Printed and bound in Great Britain by Cromwell Press, Trowbridge, Wiltshire

Note: The material contained in this book is set out in good faith for general guidance and no
liability can be accepted for loss or expense incurred as a result of relying in particular
circumstances on statements made in the book. The laws and regulations are complex and liable
to change, and readers should check the current position with the relevant authorities before
making personal arrangements.

Contents

■ ■ ■ ■ ■

Acknowledgements

■ ■ ■ ■ ■

This book has benefited from numerous discussions with friends and colleagues on the topic of 'doing a PhD', both during our doctoral study and afterwards, in the preparation of this book. We would like to thank the 30 or so current or ex-PhD students from a dozen universities who have shared their own experiences with us over the years.

In the preparation of the book itself, James Sennett took on the task of reading the manuscript with a critical eye, and we thank him for that, and for his valuable comments. We would also like to thank Treasa Creavin and Eunice Maytorena-Sanchez for patiently listening to our ideas, reading drafts and making constructive comments while we have been writing this book.

This book has drawn from a diversity of experiences of higher education establishments, not least the half dozen universities that we have studied or worked at between us. Having said that, the university where we both did our PhD has a special place in inspiring and informing the book, which, of course, could not have been written without our having got through our own doctorates. And central to *that* were our PhD supervisors, who we would like to thank for their exemplary contributions in their many roles, including encouraging the creative environment in which ideas – such as the idea for this book – could take root.

Preface

■ ■ ■ ■ ■

This book is a PhD companion – or at least the closest you will get to one without having someone follow you everywhere – and it's a companion that fits in your pocket, tells you things you need to know, doesn't assume you're superhuman, and is alive to the fact that while doing a PhD might be fun, it is also hard work, and can get a bit messy. This particular companion doesn't answer back either. It does not list rules and regulations – those vary from place to place, so you should read your university's Guidelines for Doctoral Students (or whatever they are called). They are free, after all. Nor does it tell you how to do the research itself. And it doesn't even need to be read from end to end, although it can be.

What it does is this.

It explains the processes and experiences of doctoral study, from the PhD student's point of view: the various hurdles, pitfalls, ups, downs and long boring bits that you're likely to encounter in the course of doing a PhD. It tells you roughly what to expect, and what not to expect of university departments. It tells you about the messy reality of doing a PhD, and it tells you in bite-sized chunks that you can chew over on the way to college. Of course, to ensure success, you will need time and money and a good deal of determination. You will need to take the specific advice of your supervisors and follow the regulations of your university. But this book will also help give an insight into the many things that no one ever seems to tell you, and you don't necessarily know to ask.

We wrote it because we have been through the mill ourselves. We have been, at various times in the course of our PhDs: fully funded, part-funded, and unfunded; registered, de-registered, and of decidedly indeterminate registration status; we have worked part-time, full-time and unpaid; we have changed the direction and title of our theses midstream; we have run late on drafts, chapters and submissions; we have thought about giving up, but didn't, because we couldn't think of a job that was better than doing a PhD; and we have both wished that a book like this existed, because some things that have seemingly happened to most of the PhD students we know simply aren't mentioned in any of the other kinds of guidance available.

We hope you find this book can help you with your doctoral studies.

Stephen Marshall and Nick Green

1
Introduction

■ ■ ■ ■ ■

Here we address the basics – what a PhD is, what's in it, and what's in this book.

What is a PhD?

There is a quip that when you start a PhD you know a little about everything, and by the end you know a lot about nothing. There is an element of truth in this: much of the process of doing a PhD is focusing in on a relatively small problem, and then understanding it as thoroughly as you can. In doing this, you learn how to 'do research': how to search literature critically; how to manipulate and sift large quantities of information; how to recognise and explore ideas both good and bad; how to collect data, whether from archives, libraries, interviews, or laboratories; how to develop a coherent argument from that data; how to present your research in a variety of contexts, from informal seminar to formal conference presentation; how to present your research in writing, from short working paper to your dissertation. In short, the skills required to do research for a living, should you so desire.

As much process as thing, then, the PhD is both research degree and professional research qualification. When you start a PhD, you will probably know a bit about doing a research project. When you finish, you will know a lot more about doing a research project, and much else besides.

However, pinning down what a PhD actually *is* can be surprisingly difficult, and this is even more the case with the thesis. You can think of it as the standard professional research qualification, or an 'academic passport'.

But it is also much more. You will learn a lot about yourself while doing a PhD. You'll discover strengths and weaknesses you didn't know you had, and you will probably have a hitherto unprecedented degree of intellectual and professional freedom, although this is not always the case: a 'production line' approach to their PhD students is not unheard of in some academic departments.

Doing a PhD can also be thoroughly enjoyable, even if it is plain hard work at times. You are doing something that is genuinely original, and you have control over it. Because it is often a gateway to a new career, it opens up exciting and sometimes daunting new vistas: at the end you may well find yourself headed in a direction that was far, far from your thoughts when you started.

Finally, although you might decide in the end that a career in academia isn't for you, the skills that you learned along the way are highly transferable, even if the subject matter to which you applied them in the course of your PhD is somewhat arcane.

A brief history of the PhD

The word 'doctor' is believed to have originated at the University of Bologna in the twelfth century. However, it was in Germany that the doctorate as the ultimate research qualification was effectively established. Specifically, the modern PhD (or DPhil – both mean Doctor of Philosophy) is attributed to Wilhelm von Humboldt, at the University of Berlin in the early nineteenth century. From this evolved the modern PhD we see around the world in all its variants.

Originally, Philosophy was the least prestigious of the four traditional university faculties, the other three being Theology, Law and Medicine. However, following modernisations of the nineteenth century a holistic kind of 'philosophy' led to the PhD becoming a 'badge of research excellence' across a wide range of disciplines. This kind of PhD spread to the USA (1860) and to the UK in the early twentieth century (1917).

The first PhD in the United States was awarded to James Morris Whiton, at Yale University in 1861. Whiton only did one year of doctoral study and his thesis was only six pages along (albeit in Latin) on the proverb *Brevis vita, ars longa*. Sadly for today's PhD students, things have changed a bit since then, and both time and thesis are now much, much longer.

Indeed, the fact that the PhD effectively is a product of diffusion that can be traced to a single source means that in a sense all the different kinds of PhD available around the world can be almost seen as part of the same evolutionary tree, despite differences in detail. What this means is that although there is a variety of different paths to getting a PhD, the experiences along the way will have much in common. For example, in the United States there is a significant taught element that is not required in the UK. So while a PhD can be completed more quickly in the UK (the focus of this book) by virtue of the different procedures, the experience of writing a thesis, or trying to explain your obsession to someone, is very much a common one, and much of the advice herein will cross borders that the collegiate rules may not.

A PhD route map (and guide to this book)

Like the PhD itself, this book has a rough chronology; that's to say it starts at the beginning, says what it has to say, and stops when it gets to the end. However, while it can be read from end to end, beginning with the first page, ending with the last, it need not be. Just dip into it if you want to find out about something in particular, and follow up the cross-references to find out more.

Our depth of treatment varies according to topic. If the university rules and regulations are likely to cover a particular topic better than we can, we will tell you roughly what to expect, and suggest that you read the rules. This variation in depth of treatment also reflects the relative importance of the different facets of the PhD experience of the student, as opposed to giving uniform advice on, for example, how to do research or write academically. We have tried to capture many of the things – often small but unsaid things – that we feel offer insights and shortcuts that can help the reader avoid learning the hard way or reinventing the wheel.

One thing you will need to include in your thesis is a 'strategic outline', so here is an illustrative example: it's a plan of this book.

Chapter 2 deals will all the things you need to consider before *Embarking on a PhD* while Chapter 3 introduces *Your supervisor*, the person who will be your guide through this process, and who may well have influenced your decision to do a PhD in the first place, even if from afar.

Chapter 4, *Finding Your Feet*, is to do with things like finding a desk, your position in the department, and generally finding your feet in your first year, and Chapter 5 is about actually *Doing the Research*. While it is your supervisor's job to advise on the details of your topic, this gives advice on the various research processes and procedures that you will encounter prior to writing up.

Of course the PhD experience is not just about doing a doctorate, and Chapter 6 deals with *Life as a PhD Student*. As you might expect, it is to do with extra-curricular activities, midterm blues, and other more general things that can occur at any stage – relationships for example.

Chapter 7, *Academia*, is to do with how your doctoral research contributes to your wider academic pursuits, and vice versa, and Chapter 8 returns to the PhD itself with some advice on *Thesis Construction* – this covers everything about writing up research and forming your 'thesis' (argument).

Chapter 9, *Survival*, addresses the period when life as a PhD student and writing up become tangled up, and when the going gets tough. Chapter 10, *The End Game*, deals with the specifics of producing your 'thesis' in the sense of preparation and submission of the exam script itself, that is, the thesis that you will have to defend in your viva. This takes us to Chapter 11, *The Examination*, and this covers everything from choosing your examiner to the day of the viva.

Chapter 12 deals with *The Afterlife*: the formal completion of the PhD, and ways of taking your PhD work forward. This chapter is followed by a short appendix which gives contact details for the main UK funding bodies, along with other useful information.

2
Embarking on a PhD

Here we address the most basic questions facing any would-be PhD student. Why do one? Where, how, and with whom? How to fund it and how long will it take?

Wanting to do a PhD

If ever the difference between 'liking the idea of doing' something and 'wanting' to do it is to be cleared up in the head of someone, then it is in the doing of a PhD. Wanting to do a PhD is essential to getting the thing, because there will be times when all you have to drive you is a visceral, gut-wrenching need to do it. There is a certain desperation in the successful PhD student, a blinkered obsession with it, a mindset that leads the unfunded doctoral candidate to ask not 'why I am I doing this?' but 'how can I carry on?'. There is a bike-racing book from the 1970s that points out that if you have to ask yourself what sacrifices you have to make to win, you're already losing races. So it is with a PhD: you won't notice the sacrifices if you're determined to get it, because to you, they won't be sacrifices.

But you do need to think about this. A recent survey in the USA found that three-quarters of PhD students did not reconsider their decision to embark on a PhD. This means, of course, that a quarter did have some reservations or would do it differently. Indeed, almost half of respondents said that they would or might select a different university, and further proportions would consider selecting a different supervisor or thesis topic. So, while there is a good chance that you know you want to do a PhD – and will not regret it if you do take the plunge – there is a fair chance that you might not necessarily pick the ideal topic in the ideal department if you leave things to chance.

So in the end whether or not sacrifices *feel* like sacrifices depends not only on your desire to do the PhD, but also on the environment in which you are doing it. Leaving your old university in a city that you have come to know and love will certainly be a bittersweet experience. But if you move to a new university that for whatever reason is simply not for you, then you are likely to find things difficult. The same can be said about choosing the wrong subject. What that means is that no matter how much you want to do a PhD, the environment you end up doing it in is hugely significant too. And if you are wavering anyway, going to the wrong or right place will probably make up your mind for you (see also Chapter 3).

Why another degree?

Before embarking on a PhD – indeed, well before filling in your first application form – you must carefully consider why you want to do it. In the course of several years in pursuit of the thing, the chances are you will find yourself asking how on earth you got yourself into this in the first place.

A yet higher degree

The reasons for doing a PhD are in some respects similar to those for doing any kind of postgraduate study: you may simply wish to get a higher qualification than the one you already have. If this has seemed like a good reason since your schooldays, you may feel it remains equally valid when considering doing a PhD. The phrase 'because it's there' springs to mind.

Moving into a new area

Another reason for postgraduate study is as a sideways move: to get a qualification in a different discipline. This may be appealing or necessary because your first degree was some embarrassingly unsuitable subject that you fancied when you were 16, or because it was the only course you could get into, or because – although a good bet for a cushy undergraduate life – it more or less renders you unemployable now. In other words, you think that doing a postgraduate degree in a different subject will be a springboard into a new career.

For example, the graduate of some supposedly unsexy technical discipline might try to cast their career in an exotic new direction by taking up a Masters in the History of Technology; or an engineer might seek the aplomb of an MBA to complement their sturdy Bachelor status. On the other hand, an arts graduate who can't find a job as a municipal philosopher or aesthete-in-residence might consider retraining in IT.

For the prospective PhD candidate, the chances for changing discipline are especially good, because to the extent that a PhD is an original piece of work, you are likely to be involved in cutting edge or inter-disciplinary research that nudges you towards entering a new discipline, or even inventing one. A thesis linking the evolution of the city and the physiology of the slime mould could be the start of some new field of Urbionics. Novel disciplinary permutations such as Astrosociology and Nanotheology will presumably have to start somewhere, and a PhD seems as good a place as any to make the first move.

Employability

If you are going straight to PhD after Bachelors or Masters, consider how this will affect your marketability in your next job. If your next job is outside academia, you may (in some professions) appear to be overweighed with academic qualifications relative to 'real world' job experience. On the other hand, if you definitely envisage an academic career, you will be taking the most direct possible fast track to building up an academic track record (certainly research experience, preferably publications and possibly part-time teaching experience).

A PhD can be very useful in setting you up in a career, academic or otherwise. A recent study of PhDs in USA found that employment prospects for PhD holders were very good, with an unemployment rate of less than 5%. However, it may take longer to find employment than previously, and employment may be of a temporary nature or not directly in the desired field. Indeed, the study suggested a new status quo in which many, if not most, PhD holders would not become full tenure-track faculty members. This likelihood varies by discipline and the structure of the 'industry' to which graduates are prepared.

To some extent a PhD is like a rite of passage; to some extent it is a statement of ambition. It's a bit like an undergraduate degree in this sense. Many businesses will hire university graduates, not because they need someone who has studied a particular arts or science, but just because they want someone who has been through the university thing; some degree of life experience and application (and ambition, and goal-achievement).

Some more reasons

Further favoured reasons for embarking on any postgraduate degree include: because you can't think of what else to do; you've nothing else lined up; or, simply, because you can. Some simply like the idea of being titled 'Doctor' – though there must be easier ways of picking up a few extra letters to go with your name. For those who get funding, doing a PhD may actually represent an increase in income – though others who give up jobs to get a doctorate will have to take a pay cut, and many more will actually have to run a deficit to pursue their dream.

There is a host of other more personal and idiosyncratic reasons for embarking on a PhD – perhaps not for everyone to try. Some may fancy the idea of returning to university for the promise of some kind of rarefied social life – it has been known for individuals to embark on a PhD in pursuit of their life partner – though the chances that the social life is not so much rarefied as non-existent must also be accounted for; and the chances of doctoral study actually damaging your relationships can't be ruled out either.

Whatever reason or reasons you choose for doing a PhD, it is as well to get them clear, as they could be the making or breaking of your doctorate. When the going gets tough, you may find yourself having to revisit them, as you face the possibility of deciding whether to continue – whether you need a good reason to soldier on, or a conclusive excuse to quit. Reasons like 'because it's there' or 'because I can' might not necessarily be the most helpful in those circumstances.

And if you change your objectives or priorities in the course of your thesis, you may end up taking longer than expected – especially if you end up working through the whole list, starting with the most vague or least important (see below).

Possible reasons for doing a PhD

■ To obtain a higher degree than the one you have.

■ To move into a new discipline.

■ To gain a specific training in research methods or writing.

■ To attempt to achieve a specific research result.

■ To provide a foundation for an academic or other career.

■ To immerse oneself in academic or personal study.

■ To experience or extend life as a postgraduate student.

Reasons rarely heard for doing a PhD

■ To learn how to teach students or administer university courses.

■ To spend more time with your family and friends.

■ To get rich quick.

How long will it take?

As every PhD student knows, it only takes two years to do a PhD: your first year and your final year. The first year takes at least 24 calendar months, and involves a long period of 'just starting' and faffing around wondering what you are supposed to be doing. Then, you realise you have to write up. You then fast forward to your final year, which usually takes at least another 24 months, if not more...

The great imponderable, this question. Notwithstanding our opening observation, the rules have been getting tighter over the last few years as numbers have increased and funding has become more stretched, and for this reason you should check out the requirements of both your college and your funder. In the United Kingdom the short answer is, notionally, three years studying on a full-time basis, or five years part-time. That, typically, is how long a grant is given for, and what your university will expect. The research councils which provide the funding for many PhDs have been tightening their own expectations and the percentage of people submitting within four years has increased dramatically in the last decade or so.

This is particularly the case in the social sciences and the arts and humanities, both traditionally notorious for a high rate of attrition. So whereas in the 1980s roughly 30% (within both fields) submitted their thesis within four years, the figure is now well over 70%.

So while the notional three years is more usually a minimum – although it is imposed more strictly by some institutions than others – the average length of time comes out at much more than three years. At the extremes, we know of one person who took two-and-a-half years from starting to getting the certificate, and of someone else who submitted their thesis some 18 years after starting. The more typical pattern is three years studying full-time, and then a year or more completing it while doing another job, be it post-doctoral research or in some other field. (See also When will you finish?, in Chapter 6.)

This all assumes that you will be studying on a full-time basis, or at least trying to. If you decide to go the part-time route, whereby you study while you work, you can expect to be in for the long haul. The typical length of part-time research council funding is five years, rather than three, and as the full-time period gets somewhat distended, so it is with part-time study, only more so: five to ten years is a realistic timetable.

The part-time option

If you decide to go down this road, you should expect a tougher journey than the average PhD student has, and of course, a longer one.

Part-time study has its advantages, of course. First of all, you keep your job, and therefore your connections with current developments in your field. Your professional work and your PhD topic will probably be connected – it is much, much easier if they are – and each can benefit from the other: intellectual insights from the PhD might inform your 'day job', while the practical necessities of working in the 'real world' can help keep you focused on making your research useful. In short, it puts you in a potentially strong position when having to answer the question 'what's the point of your research?' So what of the disadvantages?

Balancing time becomes paramount. The first thing to note is that whatever you spend the most time on will feel like your job. So if you work three days a week on your job and two days a week on your PhD, your job will dominate, and the PhD will be something that has to be fitted around the job. If you work two days a week on your job, and three days a week on your PhD, your PhD will dominate, and your job will become a means of paying the bills, and staying in touch with the 'real world'. But your PhD will probably become the more central task.

Even then, this is a tricky proposition. The advantage of doing a PhD full-time is that you can explore ideas and intellectual areas that might appear to lead nowhere; often that is where the most exciting discoveries are to be found. And if you find nothing, then it does not matter so much – you have the time to look elsewhere (assuming that you do not spend *all* of your time exploring fruit-less dead-ends). But when studying part-time, there are reduced opportunities to take those sorts of risk; you must be focused pretty much all of the time, and creating situations where you can expect the unexpected becomes far less practical.

What all this means is that time becomes a hugely important *part* of the research process, rather than a context within which you do it. If you have a talent for multi-tasking, then it will be refined; if you do not, you'll quickly acquire the basics!

So the million-dollar question: is it worth studying part-time? The answer is yes, but only if you are committed, well-organised and focused. If you are not all of these things, then consider a full-time solution.

■ ■ ■ ■ ▬▬▬▬▬▬▬▬▬▬▬▬▬▬▬▬▬▬▬▬▬▬▬▬▬

Albert Einstein

Albert Einstein is well known for having fitted in some of his life's greatest works while working as a humble patent officer in Bern (1902–1909). During this period he wrote an important paper on Brownian motion and two landmark papers on special relativity, that effectively made his name. During this period, in what was almost by comparison a footnote in his career, Einstein also squeezed in a PhD. He gained his doctorate from the University of Zurich in 1905, with a thesis on a new determination of molecular dimensions. Einstein was awarded the Nobel Prize for Physics in 1921.

What topic?

Unless the scope of your doctorate is specified in advance as a part of a pre-defined studentship, you are likely to have a great deal of freedom in choosing your PhD topic.

Your choice will depend on what you want to put into it and what you want to get out of it. That is, there will be a balance between the self-indulgence of choosing your favourite 'hobby' to research at doctoral level, versus doing something that could realistically speaking be writing your own future job description, or a research agenda for an academic career.

To the extent that a PhD thesis is a research training, it is the research training process that counts, rather than the research product itself. You could probably do a PhD on how paint dries (and possibly even on *watching* paint dry), or on the estimation of the number of angels that could dance on the head of a pin (an epistemological study from a critical analysis of the literature of angels and pin-heads, of course). As long as there is a valid piece of research going on, the topic itself should be fair game – at least for studying, if not for getting funded.

So, while some PhD topics may seem far-fetched, it is not to say that the doctorate is of questionable value, since the value added is in the graduate – as with any other educational qualification.

Some interesting PhD topics

- Stoic wisdom

- The physiological effects of transcendental meditation

- The suburban culture of the donut store

- Artificial animals for computer animation

- Human sexuality and extended spaceflight

- Semiotic analysis of chatroom conversation

- Elvis as postmodern Messiah

- Linguistic differences in texts produced under examination and non-examination conditions

- Blondes as both derided and desirable

- The PhD as a learning process

The Grand Academy of Lagado

On his Travels, Gulliver describes a visit to the Academy of Lagado, and the outlandish research experiments being carried out there. These include the description of a man engaged for eight years in a project to extract the sunbeams from cucumbers, with the intent of warming the air in 'raw inclement summers'. Another researcher was attempting to make gunpowder out of ice, and an architectural researcher was endeavouring to invent a method of building houses from the roof downwards. This passage is supposed to be an allegorical account of Swift's visit to the Royal Society in 1710. History did not recount how many of these research projects involved PhD candidates, or if any of them succeeded.

Funding

The most pressing problem for any student is usually funding, and PhD students are no different in this respect. Where they do differ, though, is that postgraduate funding regimes vary according to discipline. So a PhD in the natural sciences may well come with funding – if you get the place, you get the money – whereas one in the humanities might require the student to apply for their own funding; so you may get offered a place, but you then have to find a way of paying for it.

In the UK, the first place to look for funding is the Research Council most appropriate to your discipline. The Research Councils are actually part of the same body, but they act autonomously, and each Research Council has its own rules, regulations and procedures. Intriguingly, they each hand out grants of different sizes, depending on which Research Council it is, so you should expect to hear a variety of different figures for the annual grant. Such a grant should cover both fees and living expenses, incidentally. The department to which you are applying should be able to help you out here, but be aware that the whole process is intricate and time-consuming, so you should be exploring your options a good year before you wish to start your PhD.

The colleges and universities themselves will also award the occasional scholarship, and these are certainly worth investigating too. Bear in mind, though, that the competition for these can only be described as fierce in the extreme.

If you are aiming to study abroad, whether in the UK as a foreign student, or as a UK student abroad, you should find out what funding options are available, whether from your national government, philanthropic organisations, or other funding sources. You can also contact the embassy of the country to which you wish to go and ask them for advice. Of course this is all more easily said than done, so besides contacting the official organisations, you should ask around informally to see what's available and then follow up any leads.

One other source of funding is industry. Here the money might come as a 'top-up' grant or an equipment grant – it is unlikely to cover all of your fees and living expenses. But what you need to know is that such extras come with strings attached – the funder will want something back from the research, and they will probably want to stipulate what that something is. This is a matter for negotiation between the industrial partner, your supervisor and, ideally, you.

The importance of getting this right cannot be overemphasised. A failure to come to an agreement can result in the rapid collapse of the entire PhD, whereas a successful partnership can bring more than just financial benefits to the PhD: a greater practical relevance that might enhance your job prospects in industry, should you choose that route, or a valued collaborator for future academic research projects.

This all sounds like common sense, and it is. You might get lucky without effort, but you mostly have to make your own luck. If you are determined, then you will find enough funding to get you through, even if that means working to pay your way. Last but not least, and *especially* if your discipline lies in the arts and humanities, don't expect it to be easy (see also Chapter 6, Working while you study).

Where to do it?

'If the graffiti in the toilets at — is anything to go by, you'll find that these elite institutions aren't half as good as they pretend to be.' So said a friend who lectured at one such institution on hearing that one of us had won a place to go and read for a Master's degree at another such institution.

If your current institution cannot give you what you want, then it's time to move on, and that means doing a lot of homework on what's available and where. You can take it as read that every institution will claim to offer a thriving and vibrant research culture that pushes the boundaries of human knowledge, but there's no failsafe way of checking these claims. Just be aware that since these claims are the rough academic equivalent of marketing devices, there is a certain amount of hyperbole involved.

If you want to work with a particular supervisor, then you should contact the relevant department and find out how to go about applying to do a PhD. You will have to fill in an application form and should that be accepted, attend an interview.

Changing institutions

You will probably go through this process with a variety of institutions (including your current one if you are already in one) and if all goes well, you will be in the happy position of having to choose where to study next. However, you should bear in mind that it is also the case that the higher your expectations of the institution, the more likely you are to be disappointed.

There are various reasons for this. Leaving one good university in a large city to go to a more venerable university in a somewhat smaller city may initially look like moving from a large impersonal sort of place to somewhere smaller, cosier and friendlier. But while some find such an atmosphere cosy and friendly, others can feel stifled by the expectations of a place steeped in tradition, and with its own seemingly arcane sets of rules and mores. In such instances the culture shock can be considerable. And it works both ways, especially if you move to or from a capital city such as London. If you like London, and you leave it, there is a real possibility that nowhere else will quite match up to it. But if you hate London – plenty of people do – then a smaller provincial university could be (probably literally) a breath of fresh air.

Equally, going to a university in a large city from a university with a more intimate atmosphere may turn out to be plain depressing as you confront what feels like the wearing anonymity of a capital city, or a lack of tradition that makes the university feel sterile and cold. Or it could just as easily be an exciting move into pastures new. The point is, you need to do as much as you can to find out in advance: check websites; ask friends; visit the place if you can, and try to imagine yourself living there.

Whichever way you do it, the combination of making the transition from an undergraduate to a PhD student and moving to a different university in a different city can be disorientating, especially if the two universities have fundamentally different sets of traditions and outlooks. This is a real possibility if you move between one of the old 'Oxbridge' type universities and a more modern one.

Of course this is one of the reasons why you are interviewed: it gives you a chance to assess your prospective workplace. But the truth is, you'll never really know until you try it. What looks dreadful on the outside might be fantastic once you've thrown your lot in with it. And what looked like a gleaming ivory tower might turn out, for you at least, to be a gloomy coop on the inside (see also Long haul irritations; and Ten bits of advice for before you start).

Who to do it with?

Your PhD candidature and your thesis topic in particular may come into being in a variety of ways, typically somewhere between these two extremes:

- You dream up the topic of your life's work, pitch it at your preferred institution and supervisor, and it gets gratefully accepted by the university and funding body.

- An academic, typically in liaison with a funding body, defines in advance a topic for a PhD student to do, and advertises the position, which you, if you are the lucky one, get to take up.

In the first case, you choose your supervisor, whereas in the second case your supervisor chooses you. In the first case funding is not necessarily guaranteed, but may have to be negotiated separately, whereas in the second case funding is part of the deal from the start. In the first case there is more onus on you – or freedom for you – to define your own topic; in the second case the boundaries may be clearly delineated in advance, which means either the positive association of 'clear direction' or the negative ones of 'constrained path'.

Which kind you do will affect the nature of how your doctoral study unfolds, to some extent, although in practice differences between particular topics, the character of your supervisors and other circumstances are as likely to be a source of variation between PhD experiences as how they came to be set up.

If it is your own topic, then there is greater responsibility for you to communicate to your supervisor what you are trying to do, to help him or her to help you.

If it is your supervisor's choice of topic, and/or your funding body's topic, then you may find yourself having to reconcile at least two if not three different sets of objectives: your own, your supervisor's and your funding body's. While this may be a latent issue for any PhD student, it may be more likely to become acute if the PhD topic was from the start someone else's idea. These problems are also not uncommon where there is an industrial sponsor – their objectives are likely to be somewhat removed from the academic requirements of a PhD, and reconciling the two means reaching an agreement *in advance* of starting on the research itself. Such partnerships can be a great success when they work, but there is plenty of room for failure too!

A feature of being part of someone else's research programme – common in science – is that you may expect to be treated more like a member of staff with the pluses and minuses that that implies:

■ You may be expected to attend the lab all day every day unless there is a specific reason not to; you may be expected to perform communal duties around the lab, in addition to your own research.

■ On the benefit side, you may be paid better, you may get to use departmental equipment and resources as if a member of staff, and you may be invited as a matter of course to contribute to academic papers – although you may be bottom of the pecking order on all three counts.

In contrast, as a 'lone researcher' ploughing your own research furrow, you may have all the freedom to come and go as you please, without the feeling of 'reporting to' anyone, except at your own instigation; but by the same token you run the risk of becoming semi-detached from the life and work of the department.

If your PhD is a component of a larger research project or programme, you may find yourself working on a part that, frankly, no one else particularly wanted to do. This could either be because (a) it is a labour-intensive part of the work (and you are cheap); or (b) there is something a bit risky about its chance of being fruitful (in which case your dedication may have to see you through). But this scenario is, of course, no worse than if you'd thought up your topic yourself.

Ten bits of advice before you start

1. Be clear as to why you are considering a PhD.

2. Think of what career paths you might wish to follow after the PhD.

3. Bear in mind that doing a PhD can be lonely, especially when you begin, and especially if you are in a discipline that requires a lot of solitary study.

4. Doing a PhD is not just an academic enterprise. To get the best out of it (and yourself) you need to deal with the social side too.

5. When applying, try to deal directly with your prospective supervisor rather than the university's administrative channels. Check out their work, try to speak to them on the phone. Try to speak to some of their students too.

6. If you get called for interview, remember that although technically they are interviewing you, you are assessing whether or not the place and supervisor would be right for you as well.

7. Be aware that doing a PhD is quite unlike doing a taught course. A history of success in exam-passing won't cut much ice if you cannot adapt to doctoral research.

8. Be prepared for the fact that once again, you are at the bottom of the ladder.

9. Although three years may seem like a long time at the start, in the context of a PhD it is rarely enough.

10. Ask yourself why you are considering a PhD (again, just to be on the safe side).

3
You and Your Supervisor

Your supervisor is likely to be the single most significant individual in influencing the success of your PhD. Choosing your supervisor, understanding their roles – including those who are nothing to do with supervising you – and understanding their advice will be crucial to a smooth, successful PhD experience.

Your relationship with your supervisor

The dream supervisor has the following attributes: the wisdom of Solomon; a positively delphic prescience in their pronouncements of what will matter; the communicative skills of Martin Luther King; the analytical clarity of Ada Lovelace; the patience of a saint; a pastoral touch that would make Florence Nightingale weep with envy; a breadth and depth of knowledge that could only come from omniscience; creative gifts that combine the brilliance of Leonardo da Vinci, Isaac Newton, Michelangelo and Mozart with the inspiring iconoclasm of Pablo Picasso, Einstein and the Beatles; and to cap it all, an empathic sense that must have been stolen from Mahatma Ghandi.

Of course the dream supervisor does not exist, but you might well find someone who thinks they are that person, and they may well become your supervisor. The truth is that even on the rare occasions when supervisors do turn out to be geniuses, or even just very clever indeed, they are still neither gods nor saints; more likely they are simply overworked and underpaid, and just trying to do their job.

Most important from *your* point of view, they want to see you succeed. At any rate they would rather you didn't fail, because that would make them look bad. This is why: if you go off the rails, so, temporarily, does your supervisor's reputation in the department, and that means that your relationship with them is very different indeed from the average working relationship.

So here is a list of things your supervisor is (usually) not: your boss, your employer, your colleague, your best friend, your editor, your search engine, your wet-nurse. Your supervisor supervises you and your approach to your work. They don't generally tell you what to do, or what not to do, but they might warn you off some things and try to steer you towards others. As with all advice, you can take it or leave it. The pragmatic way is to take heed but not to follow blindly, for the simple reason that the types of hunch on which you might seek advice rarely lend themselves to rational explanation, but do demand careful exploration. For more prosaic or technical matters, like structuring your thesis, or getting the style right for a paper, their advice should definitely be heeded.

Your relationship with your supervisor is then subject to negotiation. One of you may want to meet once a month to discuss your progress, or you might both be quite happy to meet as the need arises. Some supervisors like to see regular progress reports, others may be less demanding, particularly if your supervisor is in regular contact with you anyway, in the lab for example. Likewise with the work itself: some students like to be given a clear sense of direction, and often; others prefer to be left to their own devices. Whatever the case may be, the important thing is to sort it out, or come to some sort of agreement as soon possible, or misunderstandings and mutual disappointment will follow. You could do worse than make the first move yourself in this respect; much of doing a PhD is about being prepared to take the initiative, and doing your best to generate a good relationship with your supervisor is as good a place to start as any.

Certainty is something you should not expect, so a key thing is to schedule in quality time for proper discussion. Supervisors tend to be busy people, and the cheery person who said hello to you in the corridor might well be a distinctly harrassed individual when you knock on their office door, asking for a quick bit of advice. If you're lucky, the cheery person will still be a cheery person, stop whatever it is they're doing, listen attentively, and then give you an absolute gem of a suggestion. More likely, they'll ask you to make an appointment so that they can be sure to give you their full attention.

How to address your supervisor

This is a great one for catching people out, combining as it does the personal preferences of the supervisor with the cultural origins of the student.

In the end, it's between you and your supervisor, but the safest route in the first instance is to address your supervisor by title – Professor Smith or Dr Jones – rather than their first name. That way, if that's what they prefer, you have got it right. But if you have got it wrong, you've simply been a little overpolite, and they will suggest a more informal mode of address. Either way, no harm is done.

Expectations: you and your supervisor

What you can reasonably expect of your supervisor

- A proper reading of work you have submitted to them.

- Timely and constructive feedback on work submitted.

- A willingness to listen to and engage with you intellectually.

- Administrative responsibilities properly and promptly addressed.

What your supervisor can reasonably expect of you

- Keep appointments.

- Try to address what the supervisor advises.

- If you disagree with them, have a good argument to back up your point.

■ If you do not understand any advice, ask for further explanation, and don't just disappear in fright/in a huff.

■ Do not overburden them with too many similar drafts – they will not be able to cast a fresh eye over it after the second draft.

■ Administrative responsibilities properly and promptly addressed.

Supervisors: the good, the bad, and the ugly

The good

The supervisor who just let their student get on with their project, offered useful advice when it was sought, *never* said they were too busy, and never asked for authorship rights on any papers published, but did send a note saying 'Congratulations!'

The bad

The supervisor who asked a student to redraft a chapter over a dozen times, including making additions that the supervisor had previously asked them to omit, and omitting work that the supervisor had previously asked them to include. In the end, the student, utterly exasperated, laid out all of the drafts on the supervisor's desk and invited them to pick one for inclusion in the thesis.

The ugly

The supervisor who could not agree on who should be first-author on a paper to be co-authored with their student, nor on what the balance of the thesis should be. This forced the student to abandon this particular line of research, start another one, and then cobble together a thesis from the debris. To the student's credit, they got the PhD.

Relating to your supervisor's research

As well as taking you on as someone paying to be educated, your supervisor might also be pleased to welcome your research activity for a variety of other reasons.

- It may extend their own research methods into new areas.

- It may treat a particular area in more depth, or help improve a method.

- It may help fill in substance to an area currently claimed in outline but only sketchily secured as part of their grand vision.

- It may go off at a tangent but help link to another topic.

In other words, your supervisor is not just there to help you deliver 'your baby': your research and your supervisor's are both part of a larger research universe. Understanding how your research relates to your supervisor's interests and priorities will also influence the way you are steered through the process: whether you are kept on a 'long leash' or a 'short leash' may not just be a personality thing.

Ten questions to ask a prospective supervisor

1. What sort of monitoring regime (eg frequency and type of meetings; progress reports and so forth) do you prefer?

2. Is there a procedure within the department for how authorship and co-authorship is decided?

3. Could I speak to some of your students?

4. Do the PhD students here socialise together (this tests his/her knowledge of what's going on in PhD-world) and what role do they play in the departmental research culture?

5. How might the PhD be funded?

6. How does my proposed topic fit with the other research you have done? How can it build on existing in-house data/methods or how could it contribute to them?

7. Who else might be an expert in this topic, to whom you would recommend I speak?

8. What institutional support is there for training/ language tuition/ travel grants etc?

9. What kind of computer facilities are available to me?

10. Where would my desk/bench be?

Lastly, and not a question: take a look at your prospective supervisor's books or papers to get a feel for their work, and where they're coming from.

Supervisors: when things go wrong...

If you are very unlucky (and leaving aside personality clashes) then you may get a supervisor who falls far short of what you can reasonably expect of them. There are various courses of action in such circumstances, all unpleasant. The first, and most likely one if you are just starting out, will probably be to try to weather the storm, and work around the problems, perhaps by relying more on your second supervisor to take up much of the slack.

Sometimes, though, things just don't work out with your supervisor, no matter how much effort you make. If you are brave, then you can politely express your concern that the relationship is not working out (they may of course feel the same way). If you cannot negotiate a more effective working relationship, then you are faced with the last resort of parting company with your old supervisor and finding a new one.

Changing a supervisor is like throwing away the rudder of a boat, so it's as well to have some sort of replacement lined up so that you can get back on course reasonably quickly. Depending on your department and your university, changing a supervisor will involve jumping through a variety of administrative hoops, so you should do some homework on what might be involved before taking any positive steps.

You will probably upset or annoy people along the way, so you shouldn't expect an easy ride; it is best to avoid it in the first place if at all humanly possible. Chances are, such a depressing scenario won't come to pass; just be aware that it could. Most likely, you will have a typical working relationship with your supervisor – variously encouraging, challenging, enlightening and ultimately successful when you get the PhD.

Loss of a supervisor

The death, dismissal or other sudden departure of a colleague, friend or boss can be unsettling at the best of times, but when the person concerned happens to be your PhD supervisor, the consequences for your own fortunes may be particularly acute.

Most likely, you will lose your supervisor because they retire or because they leave academia; these eventualities can be planned for, but are still disorientating for the student, whose own present is now firmly in the ex-supervisor's past. It is not unknown for students simply to be left to fend for themselves. If your supervisor moves to a different university, you might simply have to follow them, but at least it's up to them to sort out the subsequent mess.

In all cases, the first thing you should do is seek guidance if it isn't promptly offered (which it should be, but as with so much, you can't count on it). If both of your supervisors leave or retire at the same time – it has happened – you should start at the top, with the head of research or the head of the department and take it from there. Do bear in mind that if your supervisor has left the department, the department may well be without the one expert who understands your work. So be prepared to explain your situation to them, and again, try to offer suggestions for suitable replacement supervisors. These may well include established academics with a successful track record in supervision who know little about your subject area, but who know a PhD thesis when they see one, and with whom you think you can work successfully.

If you find yourself in this predicament towards the end of your PhD, then the question of examiners also arises (see Chapter 11, Choosing your examiners).

Disputes

Disputes arise in all walks of life, but they can be particularly acute when they involve the asymmetric power relationship that you have with your supervisor.

If a personal or professional dispute happens to you, the first thing to do is talk to someone about it, preferably at an informal level, and outside your department. Discuss the issue with your friends and perhaps certain colleagues, and they will be able to help you clarify the nature and extent of the problem. If you decide that it *is* a problem, and that it cannot be solved by informal means, then you will have to go through formal channels and that means building up a case based on evidence of specific incidents. At a formal level, your college or university will have mechanisms through which you can seek advice on what action you should take (or are in a position to take) and they will be able to assist you in taking that action. Lastly, do not wait for the problem to go away but try to deal with it immediately.

Intellectual property issues

An unpleasant anecdote tells the story of a PhD student who was blessed with a talent for having plenty of new ideas for research projects, and whose supervisor took those ideas, and turned them into research projects. All well and good, you think; that must have enhanced the reputation of the PhD student no end.

Well, it would have done, if the supervisor hadn't taken all the credit for the ideas himself. But he did. Result: a poisoned relationship and an embittered PhD student. Should the student have kept the ideas to himself, guarding them jealously? Perhaps yes, in this case.

Sadly, the truth is that the area where the balance of power between student and supervisor becomes most prominent is in the area of intellectual property. It is an issue most likely to surface when potential publications come into the picture, particularly in the 'publish or perish' environment of modern academia. And as with so much about doing a PhD, the heart of the issue lies with your supervisor. Some supervisors are happy enough to simply congratulate you if you get something published – they won't ask to be a co-author on your paper, nor will they try to hijack the ideas. They will simply give credit where it's due. Others will take the opposite approach, refusing to let you publish if they are not put down as the lead author, even if it is your idea, researched, written up and eventually submitted by you.

The problem is that the exploitative use of a research student's ideas by their supervisor will quickly lead to a breakdown of trust and so jeopardise the PhD itself. But it is also the case that in academia the race to publish is ever more competitive; this is especially the case in the life sciences, where the race might be to uncover a specific answer to a specific problem. This is less likely to be a problem in the humanities, where (usually) there is no 'right answer'.

For this reason, you should sound out *in advance* how any ideas that you have will be used and attributed, whether in papers or research proposals. If you get it right, both of you will benefit, if you get it wrong, you will probably wind up the loser.

Cecilia Payne

Cecilia Payne has been credited with writing the most brilliant astronomy PhD of the 20th century. Born in England, she completed her Bachelor's degree at Newnham College, Cambridge, before moving to Harvard to pursue a PhD. Her thesis, the first in astronomy to be awarded by Harvard, argued among other things that the bulk of the universe is made up of hydrogen. An outrageous proposition then (and now accepted as orthodoxy), she was advised by her supervisor to include in the conclusions of her thesis that her findings were probably wrong.

There is more though. The leading astronomer of the time, Henry Norris Russell, wrote to Payne that, despite the dissertation's evident brilliance, the idea that hydrogen could be so overwhelmingly prevalent in the universe was simply wrong. But a few years later, Russell wrote a lengthy paper setting out the argument which he had previously dismissed, and only towards the end did he credit Payne for her part in this work. He made no mention of his earlier rejection of this notion, and he also took the credit.

Payne's story had a happy ending though. Well, of sorts. She did, eventually, become a professor, but not until the 1950s. And in 1977, she was awarded the prestigious Henry Norris Russell prize for astronomy.

4
Finding Your Feet
(and a Desk to Put Them Under)

In the first part of your first year, your brain will be mightily stretched, not so much with the philosphical part of your doctorate as sorting out the mundane necessities of academic life – pens, paper, where to get lunch, deskspace – that sort of thing. Read on to find out roughly what to expect.

Your place in the department

In order to do a PhD, you may have had to cross oceans, (re)learn a language, sit skills tests, chase visas, convincing one country to let you leave, and another country to let you in. On top of that, you may have had to jump through more academic hoops and skillfully negotiate more regulations and departmental politics than an average established academic has to do to get a research grant of ten times the value. And all that just to get here.

On the other hand, you might have simply risen up through your department, to find a PhD studentship just waiting for you.

Either way, you're still a student when you're doing a PhD; a graduate student admittedly, but a student nonetheless. So where you sit in the departmental hierarchy is determined to a considerable degree by this simple fact. Especially if your research topic is obscure, you may be defined less by your technical field and more by whose student you are (that is, which supervisor you 'belong to').

The fact that you are *technically* a student does not necessarily correlate with how you are likely to be treated, either by staff members or by other students. One group of students – all studying within the general field of life sciences – felt that they were treated no differently than post-doctoral researchers. They certainly were not made to feel that they were students.

However, another department, in the general field of the humanities, drew the observation that even if you have had a successful professional career, are a mature student with a family, and are in your early 30s, you still get treated like an undergraduate; that is, it is assumed that you will be irresponsible, childish and ill-disciplined. Needless to say, this sort of attitude causes a great deal of resentment and does little to foster a lively research culture.

The simple fact of the matter, though, is that no matter what you have done before, once you *become* a PhD student you will be *judged* as a PhD student. Your past history will, for the most part, be irrelevant. For example, we were told of one mature PhD student who had returned to study after setting up and running a successful hi-tech manufacturing company. On his first day in the lab, he was approached by a PhD student in his early 20s who had been there for a year already. The young PhD student started to give basic instruction on how to assemble a particular piece of equipment, much to the annoyance of the new PhD student who turned to his younger colleague and said 'I made these lasers – I invented them!'

The message of the story is that when you start a PhD, you leave at least a part of your professional past behind. If you originally studied as an architect, but are now studying sociology, you may still be seen within the department as an architect, but be judged as a sociologist. To be sure, the knowledge you already have will still be useful, and doubtless people will learn to call on it. But your place in the department reflects not how you see yourself, but how those in charge see you, and first and foremost, that is as a PhD student.

So if this upsets you, don't get mad, get even. Write the respect-demanding paper that your academic colleagues would love to have penned if only they had the time (which you of course do). And if that seems over-ambitious, then just concentrate on getting even by getting your own doctorate.

The academic food chain

As a PhD student, you may find yourself as high as you've ever been, but you're still only somewhere in the middle:

- professor

- reader

- senior lecturer

- lecturer

- research fellow

- research assistant

- **PhD student**

- Masters student

- Diploma student

- undergraduate.

NB: Respect and condescension can go up as well as down!

Your contribution

Although your department may sometimes act as if PhD students should be 'seen and not heard', are regarded as taking up space, and that sometimes PhD students are a drain on valuable departmental (or supervisorial) time, remember that you have certain rights and entitlements that go along with your PhD status. Not least, these boil down to the fact that you (or someone on your behalf) are paying to do the PhD. So, you are entitled to think of yourself as a client, not a parasite.

Your contribution is not only financial, but you may be an asset to the department in other ways.

- Prestige – university departments looks better for having PhD students on their books.

- CV value – your supervisor can put you on their CV as 'students supervised' – though this is most likely only to be possible to cash in on if and when you actually pass.

- Presence – generally lending an air of inhabitation to a department – this can contribute to conviviality and even passive security.

- Intellectual stimulation – contribution to seminars, brainstorming, etc.

- Last but not least, a source of labour that can help boost a department's productivity.

None of these of themselves is likely to be something that gains any degree of influence or recognition. As in any walk of life, having an exaggerated sense of self-worth won't win many favours. But simply being aware of these as items of 'bonus' value should at least make you not feel shy about demanding the basic entitlements, such as desk space, computing facilities, or tuition, that your PhD status supposedly affords.

Your space

After time and money, space is one of the most fraught topics of the PhD experience. Without a decent place to work, you may feel insecure and always on the back foot. Your 'place in the department' in psychological and self-esteem terms is hardly supported if physically you have no place in the department to call your own.

The problem is that although you may be a vital part of the department, somewhere halfway up the food chain, you are the lowest category to actually be given any formal space allocation (whether this allocation is actually nonzero or not). Therefore, space for PhD students will be lower priority than office space for academic, research and administrative staff. This is partly because compared with staff numbers or taught course students, the intake of PhD students is volatile, and could range from a roomful one year to none the next. So the PhD student is most likely to feel the squeeze.

This is unfortunate, because it tends to dissuade PhD students from coming into the department in the first place (losing some of the benefits of having PhDs around). There is a danger of a self-fulfilling prophecy: if PhD office space is so constrained and contested that students choose to work elsewhere, the space problem ceases to be an issue. This is particularly unfortunate because PhD students typically spend more time in the department than any other group; and, of all academics or students, they are the most reliant on intellectual engagement and moral support from their immediate peers within the department: staff will already have a network of peers elsewhere to draw upon, and taught course students are, well, taught.

Therefore, we suggest:

- Find out before you arrive what desk space you are likely to be guaranteed, and actual spatial pattern of working of existing PhD students (and why).

- Find out what you are officially entitled to.

- If you feel squeezed, try to make a reasoned case for more space.

It may be that the lack of space in line with increased numbers is simply an oversight, because the department has forgotten how many PhD students there actually are (and not least, because some individuals may not themselves be sure if they are still a PhD student).

Office facilities

Telephones

The advent of the mobile phone means that telephones now crop up in the most unlikely places, but getting useful access to one in an academic department can be trying. If you are doing research in the natural or life sciences, ready access to a telephone in college might not matter much, but if your research is in the social sciences, there is a good chance that at some point you will want to arrange and conduct interviews with people, and a telephone is invaluable here.

The facilities on offer vary enormously, even within faculties. Insofar as we can track down any typical rule of thumb, it is that telephone facilities are often given extremely grudgingly to PhD students, usually after lengthy negotiations, and with heavy restrictions – you are extremely unlikely to be able to make calls to foreign countries, for example. Some departments simply refuse to countenance even local calls to the outside world, although incoming calls are allowed, and this can be the case even where the majority of PhD students need access to a phone to arrange interviews. The typical strategy is simply to accept PhD phone calls as a necessary personal expense, a galling fact for foreign students in particular, who pay thousands of pounds each year in fees to study for a PhD. But to put it in some kind of context, UK universities are massively underfunded and that means that they will claw back money where they can, and as ever, it is the students, you included, who suffer.

Computers

As with telephones, computing facilities vary. And as with telephones, you cannot be sure of getting a computer: access to one, yes, but having exclusive use of one, possibly not. For the early part of your PhD, that might not matter, especially if you have ready access to shared computing facilities in a lab, for example. If your area of study is in the humanities, we would advise doing your utmost to get your own computer, especially if your department cannot or will not provide you with exclusive use of one. It need not be brand new, but you do need to know how to use it properly (one of us wrote his PhD on a ten-year old Apple Mac, the other used a miscellany of PCs at university and at home, since no single computer had the right capacity, speed, software, peripherals, 24-hour access and so on). Once you get into the realms of seriously heavy-duty computing – requiring supercomputers – then you will need to use the university's computing facilities anyway.

Once you are writing up, having ready access to your own computer will prove invaluable. There is a lot to be said for getting a laptop too: many libraries allow or encourage the use of laptops for example, and being able to work when and where you please is hugely advantageous. If you are unlucky enough to be in a department that requires its PhD students to 'hot desk' (a space saving ploy), then a laptop is almost essential.

Library privileges

As a postgraduate student, you will probably be entitled to take out more library books than are undergraduate students, but you will doubtless have to go to the library to find this out. Yet another argument for doing your homework.

Paper clips

No one will ever tell you whether or not you can use the departmental stationery cupboard, and anyway the answer you get will depend on who's doing the answering. Our advice: don't count on being able to use departmental stationery, but there's no harm in asking.

Health and safety

If you work in a laboratory, or a workshop, you will need to know about the appropriate Health and Safety regulations, since now, you're less a student who only turns up for lectures, and more akin to a full-time member of staff. Add to that the likelihood that you will be working late, when most people have left for the day, and it becomes clear that 'knowing the rules' is very much in your interests.

A fresh start

The start of your PhD is a good time to make a fresh start and get into some good habits. Now may be the time when for once in your career you intentionally set yourself up to do three or more years on a single 'project', that (unlike many an employment contract) you fully intend to see through. So, no matter how you were used to working before, doing a PhD is likely to be a good time to correct previous inefficiencies, and build in new working practices that will stand you in good stead not only for your PhD but for years to come:

■ Buy decent equipment and stationery upfront to get the most benefit from it from the outset.

■ Get into good habits of computer back-ups and virus checking.

■ Establish and maintain a consistent system of filing and bibliographic records.

■ Get into good habits of research planning and time management.

(See also Time management, in Chapter 5.)

5
Doing the Research

A PhD is fundamentally all about setting up, carrying out and writing up research. This chapter will take you through what doctoral research involves and how to do it, with some straight advice on processes and procedures; in fact, roughly everything prior to 'writing up'.

Originality and what it means

Being original is not difficult. There is a story, possibly apocryphal, that goes like this. In an engineering department in a university there is a large concrete block that has been hit with hammers numerous times, for numerous projects. And for each project it has been hit from a different angle. And, so long as that angle had not been used before, the project could genuinely be said to be an original contribution to knowledge.

In short, 'original' means simply and literally that it has not been done before. It does not mean clever, innovative, ambitious, creative, beautiful, surprising, or even unusual. Being original, by this sort of definition, isn't even difficult. It is essential though, but you will find that trying to get out of people what 'original' really means is often quite difficult.

In fact, the 'it' that has not been done before can be a variety of things besides hitting a concrete block with a hammer at a new angle. It could be using a different type of hammer, in this example, or a new type of concrete. More generally, it might be studying a new phenomenon that hasn't been studied before, or using novel techniques and approaches to study a known issue. The point is, though, that 'being original' is definitely not something you should lose sleep over.

Far more constructive is to make sure that you are *not unoriginal*. This means making sure that what you are doing is demonstrably different – however incrementally – from what has gone before. If you ensure that that is the case, you are doing something original, and you have jumped that hurdle. What you can then do is get on with learning how to do good research.

Finding that someone else has 'done your thesis'

Many discoveries are made simultaneously and independently. It comes as little surprise, then, that from time to time someone completes 'your thesis' before you do, scuppering it completely. It may be in the form of a rival PhD, or it may be a whole research team who are catching up and threatening to overtake you. But whatever form it takes, besides losing your thesis entirely, or maybe losing a supervisor, this can reasonably be called a worst case scenario.

The question is what to do about it when it happens (and how you respond will depend on when it happens). You can do a certain amount of homework yourself. The UK Research Councils all list what research grants they have given to whom, and for what purpose. The lists include grants given to large research projects as well as individuals, so a perusal of those lists may well prove invaluable (and interesting too).

At the end of the day, though, the only way you can really minimise the possibility of this happening is by doing a thorough literature review, and keeping abreast of developments in your field. You may be able to salvage the situation by changing what you're doing slightly, to re-inject a degree of originality, or you might just have to start again.

Searching the literature

Searching the literature is something that you should be doing from day one. You are required to demonstrate an understanding of the 'relevant body of knowledge' in your thesis, and this means several things. First, and most important, is that since your topic is, by definition, unique, you are the person best placed to decide what is relevant, and what is not relevant. But to be in a position to do that effectively, you must, logically, know the irrelevant stuff too.

Second, you are also required to make an 'original contribution to knowledge' so you need to know what other people have done, if you want to avoid reinventing the wheel. But despite all this, the literature review can seem somewhat pointless, something that you have to do, but that stops you from getting on with your *real* job, research.

You will probably find a degree of cynicism about the whole thing in some quarters. The definition offered by one PhD student of how to do the literature review goes something like this. First, work out what your argument is. Next, find a good range of literature that goes *against* your argument, but that is actually quite weak in terms of how it makes it case. Finally, dig out a better range of literature that supports your argument, and that is much better than the 'anti' literature. Now write it all up, concluding with the point that a thorough review of the relevant literature has demonstrated the validity of your argument.

Even within the literature concerned with the research process, you can find a certain scepticism about the true usefulness of the literature review, as this quote from *The Art of Fieldwork* by Fred Wolcott demonstrates:

> When and how theory makes its real entry into the research process is often masked by the canons of reporting. This is especially so in the constricted format of thesis and dissertation writing, in which the typically tedious review of the literature in a traditionally perfunctory second chapter includes an equally tedious recital of 'relevant' theory.

Of course, a literature review need not be mechanistic. If you want it to be, it can be a thoroughly enjoyable and absorbing enterprise, since your job, as it were, is to immerse yourself in a topic that fascinates you anyway, and to do so solidly for the best part of a year. So you might well be learning a lot, but you also have to give the review some sort of structure. At the end of it, you have to have an answer to that most difficult of questions: 'so what's your point?'.

Getting it all in focus

One of the things that can hinder your attempts to find an answer is that you will find plenty of theories and ideas, which appear, on the face of it, to be relevant. The problem is that once the veneer of superficiality has been scraped away, they turn out not to be relevant at all. And this is where the problem of finding the 'relevant' literature falls into sharp relief: large chunks of infuriatingly *irrelevant* literature have to be ploughed through to get at the truth; they must be read, or at least skimmed, digested, discussed, and ultimately dismissed, but included nonetheless to satisfy the inquiring mind (yours, in the first instance, but also your supervisor's and your examiners') which is drawn to the perfectly reasonable, but wrong, conclusion that a superficial appeal is a genuine connection.

But that's what knowing the subject is all about: knowing the limits, knowing what is relevant or is not, and being able to spot things that look *irrelevant* but are actually extremely useful. Because at the end of the day, whether you believe the cynics who believe it's a pointless exercise in jumping through hoops, or the enthusiasts who are just plain fascinated by it all, you have to review the literature. Often, it is an enjoyable experience. Sometimes it's boring. And almost certainly you will feel overwhelmed by the sheer quantity of material, the well-known phenomenon of information overload.

Information overload

In 2003, enough information was generated to fill the United States Library of Congress five times over. The amount of it that you cover, no matter how voluminous it seems, is an insignificant particle in the information universe, and the big question is how in the world can you hope to cover everything? The small answer is: you can't.

One of the things that makes reviewing the literature so difficult is that nagging away somewhere in the front of your mind, constantly, will be the fear that you have missed something vital, something of such huge import that if you miss it, your examiners will never let you forget it. So you search and you search and you search, but you don't know what for. You know you will recognise it when you find it though. And sooner or later, you will feel utterly overwhelmed by how much stuff there is. You will feel that you know nothing, absolutely nothing, even though the fact is that you know more than you ever have. This is information overload.

It might make you feel a bit better to know that you are not alone in having this problem, but it won't really help you deal with the problem, so here is some advice. First, bear in mind that you have to stop somewhere, and accept that it is genuinely impossible to cover everything. That means that you have to choose which bits to cover. You will probably find that there are relatively few works that sit right at the heart of things, and are genuinely irreplaceable. You will also find that, after a while, the same things keep cropping up, and that means that you have covered most of the intellectual ground, even if you haven't read everything written on the matter. It also means that you are starting to find themes and patterns in the literature, and that means you are making progress. So take heart at this point, you're through the worst of it.

Well, almost. Your next task is to decide which of those references are best suited to your needs, and put them to one side for the time being. You will probably feel that you are making somewhat arbitrary decisions at some point, and be unsure that you are getting it right, but that is why you just put the other stuff to one side. After all, you can always come back to it if needs be.

But as has been pointed out, there is a certain arbitrariness to the whole procedure. It is after all you who chooses which literature to include, and which to omit, and you will probably make that choice on the basis of what you are intending to argue in your thesis. It would clearly be foolish to destroy your own argument when a different choice of literature could provide a firm foundation for it; this is particularly the case in the humanities. One last thing. Information overload will make your head spin for a while, but once it has settled down again, you will find that you're much better at sorting the good stuff from the bad, and quickly. And *that* is part of doing a PhD.

PhD as jigsaw

You start with a whole load of interesting bits and pieces, that you think might some day fit together to make an interesting pattern. You fit together the pieces you have, and start looking for more pieces that might expand the whole, or fill in gaps. All the time you are doing two things – getting a physical (procedural) fit between the pieces, while building up a pattern of content or message. It can be very satisfying to build up this picture. You get to know what to look out for, and you start to scrutinise every new piece of information you come across to see if it can contribute. The tricky bits come when things just won't fit; when there are lots of similar looking bits that you just cannot decide where to put, and some bits that you later wonder if they are part of the jigsaw at all, but which you are loathe to throw away. But at the end of the day, a jigsaw – your jigsaw – must be finished; ultimately you are in control of what the pattern is, and where it starts and finishes.

Methodology: research as an iterative process

This book is clearly not about how to *do* research – there are plenty of other books on that – but there are aspects of methodology that are sometimes glossed over, or omitted altogether, and it is these more general topics that we shall look at here.

The first of these is that, despite the clarity of presentation in a journal paper or thesis about how a research project was done, be it physics or ethnography or musicology, the research process itself is actually rather messy. And although the methodology chapter in any PhD that you read will set that methodology as if it were a carefully and intricately structured plan of action, carried out with ruthless precision, there is one little word that gives the game away and tells you that things were actually otherwise. It is a word that many examiners will look for, because they want to know that you really understand what research is all about. That word is 'iterative'.

Iterative means repetitive, and in the context of a research project, it means that you will read about your topic, develop a working hypothesis, try to test it, whether through experiment, interview, archival research or by some other means, develop a tentative theory based on your findings, and then return to your hypothesis to see how your theory compares with it. Now, in the literature, the impression is given that this is all that happens in a research project, and if the research has been well designed, the hypothesis will have been properly tested. For large projects run by experienced researchers, this may well be the case for the most part, but even then, the methodology will have been tested and refined in a controlled way.

In all projects, to a greater or less extent, you will find yourself returning to the existing literature and comparing your findings and your hypothesis with it. You will then repeat the process, having refined certain aspects of your approach, and after a few cycles you will start to feel that you are getting 'proper' results.

As a consequence, you will find that your actual 'research', whether archival, lab work, fieldwork or some other information gathering process, is much messier and much more time-consuming than you expected it to be. You will probably find yourself breaking your own rules from time to time, or making new ones up. But you should know why you're doing it.

So don't worry if you feel that your methodology seems messy, and that you are not doing it 'by the book'. The important thing is to understand *why* it seems messy. The answer to that can be put quite simply: research is an iterative process. But understanding that simple fact will make it much easier when it comes to the necessary task of writing your methodology chapter, and justifying your approach to the research.

Fieldwork and lab work

Doing research is likely to involve some sort of fieldwork or lab work, from archival research in a foreign library to setting up atmospheric monitoring equipment in the Arctic Circle; from counting grass species in the middle of nowhere to counting microbes in a lab in London; from interviewing businesses in the urban hinterland to living with nomads in the Sahara desert.

What you would like to research and how you would have to research it may differ in their appeal. So the method may influence your choice of PhD topic. For example, if you love travelling, you might want to find a topic that allows you to travel widely. The point is that you should be aware of what your research will entail on a methodological basis, since it may influence the appeal of doing a PhD in the first place.

Marie Curie

Marie Curie was one of the first women to gain a PhD in science, and the first female PhD in France. She received her doctorate in 1903 with a thesis on 'Research on Radioactive Substances' – 'radioactivity' being a word of her own invention for the phenomenon of her research enquiry. Her examiners hailed it as contributing more to scientific knowledge than any previous thesis. Later that year she was awarded the Nobel Prize for Physics (jointly with husband Pierre and Henri Becquerel), and in 1911 she won the Nobel Prize for Chemistry for the discovery of polonium and radium.

Curie's scientific career is a mixture of romance and tragedy. She did some of her most important research in a 'miserable old shed', and is supposed to have fainted from hunger because she was too absorbed in her study to eat. At one point she describes how 'Sometimes I had to spend a whole day mixing a boiling mass with a heavy iron rod nearly as large as myself. I would be broken with fatigue at the day's end.' Curie is reported to have lost nearly 10 kilograms while doing her thesis research. More seriously, she suffered from radiation poisoning, that ultimately proved fatal. Even today, her notebooks are too contaminated to handle.

Time management

Time management is important for any job or project, but is especially important in the case of one that is relatively flexibly defined in a way that could end up consuming a significant portion of your life. Whole books are written about time management. Here, we just outline some of the tactics you can use to help make best use of that all too elusive commodity.

1. Set objectives and priorities

Make sure you keep an eye on the big picture, and keep things in proportion. If your objectives for doing a PhD are 90% technical and 10% networking, then by all means allow yourself to spend some of your research time networking (from emails to conferences), but don't get it out of proportion.

2. Create decent-sized chunks of time

Some big tasks need a decent amount of time to be fully immersed in. Squeeze small tasks (like filling in forms or checking your email) into small bits of time, and set aside whole days or weeks for really big tasks such as writing up.

3. Fit those chunks of time to other cycles

Allocate all those months, days and minutes to fit other cycles of the calendar (seasons and holidays), your family, friends and colleagues (weekends, eating together), to periods of waiting while experiments run their course, and your own biorhythms. Balance the most intensive or challenging activities with the times you are most alert to the task; and do more relaxing or repetitive tasks when your brain is running slower or engaged in other activities. For example, if you are going to start major surgery on a chapter, it may be best not to attempt it late in the evening, but to leave it for the next day, when not only are you fresher, but the whole day beckons for taking as long as it takes. Some other tasks, like formatting data, or messing around with diagrams, might better be done while listening to music or when you are not so hyper-alert that you get frustrated by the slowness of your computer.

4. Order the tasks to fit a critical path

Pay attention to tasks on critical paths – things that may not be overly important of themselves, but which may hold up other tasks if they are not done. Overall, sort out what are urgent and important tasks, what are urgent but not important, and what are important but not urgent, and plan so that the right ones receive the appropriate priority.

5. Make targets

Don't just plan ahead in thinking of all the tasks you have to do, but turn those into real targets, where a certain task has to be done by a certain time. Then, if the target is in danger of not being met, consider if the fault is your lack of application or an under-estimation of time, and hence how to plan better for the next target.

Targets are more easily met if they are well defined: this goes for the whole PhD. If the aim of your PhD is vaguely to immerse yourself in academia, or to lose yourself in the library, you probably will. It will be hard to judge when you get there or to judge progress on the way there, or how long it will take. If, however, your target is 'Conduct 100 interviews on the public understanding of science', at least you will have a feel for how long the whole will take, relative to the parts, and you will be able to tell as you converge towards the final goal.

If you continually shift targets, or never pin them down sufficiently, you will be in danger of drifting; research is messy enough at it is, and drifting through your PhD is a good way of failing it.

6. Tell others about your targets

Telling other people about your targets can help commit yourself to a realistic but serious programme. The ambition of meeting your stated target in front of at least one other person will spur you on to really try to hit the target. Conversely, fear of failing to publicly meet a stated target should avoid the private self-delusion of setting overambitious targets in the first place.

7. Avoid procrastination

Be aware of the things you are most likely to procrastinate on, and decide early on if it is better to drop them and do things a different way, rather than vainly hold on to the intention of doing some unappealing chore, but always putting it off.

8. Manage diversions and distractions

Diversion occurs where something unscheduled pops up to grab your attention (email for example), and since it's not in the plan, the plan goes out of the window; the chances are that it will displace some higher priority action too. If possible, put potential distractions and diversions to the side until they can be incorporated in a later part of your schedule, and accorded the correct time priority.

9. Be careful about perfectionism

In business, a general rule is to avoid striving for 100% right, when 80% right will do. Unfortunately, a PhD thesis is subject to examination, where 20% wrong won't do. Any identifiable defects will demand correction, so there is no point in cutting corners if this jeopardises the success of the whole enterprise. The trick is to identify which bits could be done more quickly, and which have to take as long as they take. This could apply to many parts of the doctoral process, even the thesis itself. A thesis that is 20% shorter may be just as good. What you choose to spend your time on will depend on your objectives and priorities (see point 1).

10. Allow yourself to overshoot

Set yourself a deadline by all means, but leave yourself room to overshoot it. One of the advantages of doing a PhD is that the deadlines for submission of work are all somewhat arbitrary, and when writing up, you can turn that to your advantage. In all likelihood, it won't actually matter if you hand in your thesis three weeks after your money has run out instead of on the day. If you hold yourself to too tight a deadline, you are more inclined to leave things out that perhaps should be included. This last is important. Ask yourself: do you want to overshoot and spend an extra day inserting that paragraph before submitting the thesis, or would you rather be told to put it in by your examiners? If you want to avoid the latter outcome, overshoot.

Time recording

Advantages

1. Knowing how long things take assists all aspects of time management and planning.

2. This helps you achieve the PhD and life priorities you invest in, in the right balance.

3. And *this* can help avoid being depressed or stressed about the passing of time.

Disadvantages

1. You might have left work (or avoided getting a job?) precisely to avoid things like time records.

2. Keeping a record of time might just make you depressed about how fast time passes.

3. Keeping a record of time might become another stressful chore/burden.

The upgrade report

One of those things that no one ever really tells you about, the upgrade report is actually the first real milestone in your PhD. It can also be a millstone that tends to loom large, by dint of its status as the only tangible mark of progress on the road to the viva.

New PhD students are typically registered to do an MPhil – Master of Philosophy – and then about a year in (give or take several months) they will upgrade their registration to that of PhD. The purpose of the process is to establish that the work you are doing and planning to do will result in the successful completion of a PhD: if this looks not to be the case, then the university is able to record a successful MPhil rather than a failed PhD. It has the secondary purpose of giving the student something concrete to focus on.

The upgrade tends to be presented as something of a formality, but despite its low profile, can dominate your thoughts in the weeks or months spent preparing your upgrade report.

The requirements for upgrading – the hoops you have to jump through – vary. They should be set out in the university's rule book, so read that first, talk to your supervisor, and then try to find out what other people had to do. Don't take this is as gospel, but typically, you will have to prepare a report, and make a brief – 15 minutes perhaps – presentation of it. The report will probably comprise a proposed table of contents for your thesis, a literature review, progress report and a plan of action for the rest of your PhD.

This is more easily said than done, since being new to doing a PhD, you won't have a great deal of confidence about how to go about planning one, especially if you are only a few months into it.

The important thing here, then, is to find out as much as you possibly can about what is required. If hard information is not forthcoming, you may have to signal this to your supervisor; make them aware that you consider the guidance given insufficient. Once you have established as far as possible what is expected, then it is your prerogative to deliver it. You will get through, and your status will be upgraded.

It is a feature of the PhD experience that you are often never quite sure that what you have done is ever enough, until the very end. In your first year or two, you may even be tantalised as to whether you have done enough even to be called a PhD candidate. Now, after the upgrade, at least you really are, finally, a PhD student.

A PhD is like a maze

When you start off, you may only have a vague idea which direction to set out in, or even how big the maze is. At the start, all sorts of possibilities open up, you turn this way and that. The walls close in on you either side. After a while, you may feel lost. You get the feeling you have been going round in circles. You wonder if you will ever find a way out.

Sooner or later, you realise that the walls are not sheer vertical faces, but have steps cut into them here and there, allowing passage up the sides of walls, which form a series of stepped terraces. After a series of false trails and reverses, you find yourself out on top of the walls. Now you can gaze out over the lie of the land of the whole labyrinth. At this point, in fact, you can visualise for the first time that there is actually a way out – along the tops of the walls.

There is still a lot of work to be done – you still have to puzzle out which way to go, and make your way there – but you now have the confidence that you can solve the maze. Eventually, after traversing the tops of the walls, you work your way out to freedom.

Knowing to look out for steps that help you scale the walls of the research maze, and knowing which kind of maze to tackle in the first place, are all part of the PhD learning process. That's why the PhD is regarded as an educational process, and not just a thesis or research output. Once you have done one PhD, you are well equipped to tackle any future research maze.

6
Life as a PhD Student

In this chapter, we look at the way in which your life out-side the PhD will be affected by the fact that you are now doing one. And believe us, it will be, so read on . . .

Long haul irritations

Culture shock

Culture shock can take a variety of forms, from trying to fit into a new national culture to trying to fit into a new university culture, to trying to fit into a new intellectual culture. You may find that guidance for doing this is severely lacking, if it exists at all, and that finding your feet can be a disheartening experience at first.

Of course, there is plenty of advice for trying to understand a new national culture: guidebooks such as those published by Lonely Planet or the Rough Guides have sections on the national culture, history, weather and a whole host of other topics, and if you are serious about going abroad to study, then it might be worth browsing through a few of those guidebooks to at least get a feel for whether your chosen country is likely to be right for you (assuming, of course, that it has the language and topics you wish to study).

As far as trying to fit into a new university culture goes, you will, hopefully, have seen your prospective new university at interview, and been shown around. Of course, while this can give you a rough idea of the type of environment you are likely to find yourself in, the fact of the matter is that you never really find out until you get there.

Our general advice is to find out what other people from your country feel about any culture shock by contacting your country's students' association in advance. In fact being aware of whether or not your intended university actually *has* a student's association/ society for your compatriots is valuable knowledge in itself.

Weather

'I still haven't got used to the weather' is a common complaint of students who come to Britain from sunnier climes. They have a point: Britain on a wet, cold Sunday afternoon in late November can be a pretty depressing place, a landscape – urban *or* rural – of drab greys and browns, capped by a pallid, overcast sky. To the average Brit this is normal, one of the reasons why pubs were invented.

The winter months, when the evenings are long and dark, can be thoroughly dispiriting. At this time of year, a drop in creativity and a decline in enthusiasm can strike hard, and because the British winter is peculiarly remorseless in its drabness, this is the time when you, as a foreign student, are most likely to feel homesick and lonely.

So while the weather might seem trivial as an issue, it really isn't: it's one of those seemingly minor things that feels insignificant for a short while. But over time, as you discover that it *won't* go away, it can *really grind you down.*

Living in English

One of the more tiring aspects of doing a PhD for students whose first language is not English is having to speak English all the time. Even those who have lived in Britain for years and have an excellent command of English say that it is a relief to be able to speak in their native language. It is an issue that often manifests itself in late-night conversations, when everyone is somewhat tired: the effort to speak in your second language can become considerable (see also Language and writing style, in Chapter 8).

When you're down

At some point, you can be reasonably sure that you will feel down. The research feels as if it is going nowhere, or it seems trivial, or it may just feel like more than you can cope with. You might wonder whether you are even good enough to be doing a PhD in the first place. You may have moved to a new university, and find it hard to fit in, as you realise that the seemingly gleaming ivory towers look rather chipped and tarnished from the inside.

If you are working on your own, rather than in a lab, say, or if there just isn't any feeling of being in a group, you may well feel isolated, misunderstood and neglected. Quite possibly you will feel uncertain too. So what to do?

First and foremost, *you are not alone!* It doesn't matter what you're studying particularly: indeed, you might be surprised by how similar are the various PhD complaints and problems amongst different disciplines. But because a PhD is often a rather solitary pursuit, you might not be aware of this.

The best way of getting proof that you are not alone is to talk to other PhD students. What you will find is that they feel the same way, and have similar problems. If there is a graduate society, join it, because there you will meet other PhD students. Even if no one actually ever talks about their PhD, the fact that you all have a PhD to *not* talk about can be a common bond which makes a welcome break from other social situations.

PhD joys: being paid to do a hobby?

A Royal Air Force pilot once remarked in a TV documentary that being a pilot was like being paid to do your hobby. A throwaway remark, perhaps, but also an apposite one, because doing a PhD can feel like that too.

When a PhD is going well, it has all the hallmarks of a hobby. It is utterly absorbing; it doesn't feel at all like work;

you don't notice the time; your everyday cares and worries are far from your mind. This might sound like hyperbole, but it is actually true. That is not to say that there won't be times when it is plain, boring hard work. But since much of this book is about what to do when things go wrong, here is some advice for when things go wonderfully right. Enjoy it!

PhD progress

You can sometimes tell the state of doctoral progress by the state of a PhD student's domestic environment. In the white heat of intellectual pursuit and discovery, things like housework may tend to fall by the wayside. But, when progress stalls, and you're having a 'bad PhD day', suddenly chores such as cleaning the windows or scrubbing the kitchen floor can become engaging, productive activities.

Meeting people

Your life as a PhD student could lead to the best and worst social life you ever have. Best, because the flexibility that a PhD affords allows you to enjoy as full a social life as you could ever wish – to party, stay up late and sleep in the next day like never before. Even as an undergraduate, there are usually fixed events like lectures to go to, whereas some PhD students can easily have days or even weeks with no definite appointments to intrude on the hedonistic time schedule. Of course, such a lifestyle may come at a heavy price, if each day spent socialising in your first year means one more day added at the end of your PhD, burdened with a late running thesis, with no time or money to socialise at all.

Surviving relationships

There is a view that says the PhD student should not get into a relationship with anyone else except another PhD student: no one else can understand, even less empathise with, what you are doing and why you are doing it. The obsessions that arise, the need to drop everything in pursuit of a promising idea, the distant gaze that periodically drifts across the PhD student's face mid-conversation, the need to work late *yet again* are all daily irritants for those around a PhD student.

In this view, the people in the best position to understand these various traits and foibles and needs and obsessions are the people who share them, the people who recognise and understand what's going through your mind because it's going through theirs too.

Of course, you don't tend to choose a partner on the basis of their abilities as doctoral counsellors, and meeting someone with a good old sense of humour and magnetic sexual attraction may be a breath of fresh air compared with someone who, like, empathises with your methodology. As with any other area of personal attraction, there is likely to be a mix of shared interests and exotic otherness.

However, it's as well to be be warned: relationships and doctoral study don't necessarily make the easiest of bedfellows (relationships with other doctoral students notwithstanding). Non-PhDs cannot be guaranteed to understand or accept what you are doing, and if you get together with someone who isn't doing a PhD, or hasn't done one, you will have a lot of explaining to do. Why, you'll be asked, are you so obsessed with this thing? Why can't it wait until the morning? When *will* you be available to go out for dinner on a weekday evening, or even a weekend? And what about the fact that now that your grant has run its course, you are living off your partner's income? When *are* you going to get a job?

Such questions are indicative of loss of patience at the best of times, but at least if your partner knows what doing a PhD is like, they will be more inclined to accept your answers to such vexed questions. Some partners are keen for you to get the PhD out of the way, and will support you in your endeavours, if only to make their own life more comfortable. Others might be more grudging, though. It's as well to remember that, what you see as a deep interest in a fascinating topic that needs all the energy you can muster, might well appear to your partner as nothing more than a thoroughly unhealthy obsession with a trivial topic that makes you a nightmare to be around.

Unpalatable truth it might be, but they have a point. *You* are the problem, certainly as far as your partner is concerned, and so you will need to compromise too. A PhD doesn't *have* to bring a relationship crashing down, but its capacity to bring considerable friction into a relationship (even with another PhD student) should not be underestimated.

When will you finish?

If you were given a pound for every time someone asked you how long it would take to finish your PhD, you would be able to pay off your Late Submission Fee.

It is probably the single most disturbing, irritatingly persistent yet witheringly damning question you will face in your time as a PhD student. Unlike a taught course, which most normal students do, the PhD does not have a fixed date of completion.

After a few years, 'When will you finish?' will hover over you permanently. It will become implicit in every conversation with your supervisor, your academic colleagues, your university administrator, maybe even your bank manager. It is a favourite of friends and family, although for them it is really an entrée into the second most dreaded PhD question, 'What are you going to do when you finish?'.

For your friends, perhaps this means 'when you will get a proper job?' so you can afford to join them for a decent meal out once in a while; perhaps for your family it's a case of wondering if they will have to make contingencies for an extended period of being sponged off, during your final year(s). It is precisely the uncertainty of (not) knowing when you will finish your PhD that heaps ignominy on your predicament. Not only will you inevitably take longer than originally planned; you don't even know how much longer, which reinforces the point that, though you are sacrificing your career and much of your spare time on some kind of labour of love, you are quite possibly not very good at it, and certainly not in control of it.

Answering the question

The key to a skilful answer, therefore, is to be brazenly confident. This can be achieved by (a) sticking to the known facts (i.e., avoiding answering the question) and (b) being brazenly confident that the PhD will take longer than anyone thought it would.

(a) Avoid prediction

A good technique for handling the future, in general, is to talk only about the past. Never refer to what you might do or achieve; only refer to what you have actually done. For example, refer to progress made (things that are satisfying and life-affirming, like books read or conferences attended) rather than things still to do (things you dread and fear, like results to be written up, or methodologies to be retrofitted). Say how long the last chapter took: don't estimate how long the next one will take. People can draw their own conclusions; if they turn out to be wrong, it is a failure of their imagination, not your inaction.

(b) Aim to be late

The question of when you will finish is painful because you always get it wrong. You always underestimate it. The only solution, then, is to overestimate it. A good trick is not to kid yourself how short a time you will take to complete your thesis: but to impress everyone else how long it will take. By putting an outrageously distant time horizon on your PhD, people will almost inevitably ask you how it can possibly take that long. You will then have to justify why it should take so long – a less disagreeable prospect than spending great time and effort trying to justify why you haven't finished yet.

In fact, explaining why your thesis will take so long is a useful (if sobering) exercise in its own right, forcing you as it does to face up to the magnitude of the task ahead. Your inquisitor will then start to wonder how on earth you are going to make ends meet for the four year over-run that your analysis implies. You too should ask yourself this question, and before the money runs out. On the whole, it is better to appear to have a herculean struggle on your hands, an exotic dragon, the slaying of which will consume the next half-decade, rather than appearing to be afflicted by a mundane but unmentionable personal demon, a debilitating Achilles heel that plagues your every waking hour.

So think of a number, double it, and add a bit more. Arranging for a heroic over-run means that any deviation from this will be an 'ahead of schedule' adjustment. Aim to be late, so that when you come in late, you are on time. (Alternatively, manage your time better in the first place – see Chapter 5, Time management).

Diminishing marginal overruns

One way of telling how close you are to completion is to track the scale of error by which you are currently over-running. At the start of your doctoral study, you may estimate three years, so by the time you start your fifth year, your estimated time to completion is already a year out. By the time you are in your final year, your estimated over-run will likely be down to being measured in months, and as you grind towards submission, you may notice that your latest estimates are only running weeks late. Sooner or later, you will get it down to days, and finally, your prediction will match exactly your completion.

Working while you study (or, in search of cash and kudos)

Whatever else you do in your time as a PhD student, you must exploit the status it affords as much as possible. Let's face it: you may be a bankrupt nobody, but your university may be rich and prestigious. By association, you may be able to appear more respectable and trustworthy than your financial status would otherwise indicate.

An excellent way of doing this is to get a job – any job – in the university. This means that you can always be ready with the handy bluff that you 'work at the university'. Even if you are just sorting the mail, the status associated with work will open many more doors than being a student, especially with irritatingly curious people like prospective landlords. They always want to know what you do. Even though you may be a mature 30-something who already had a successful career in a respectable industry, for some the simple word 'student' can conjure up nightmarish visions of a juvenile cocktail of vice, vomit and vermin.

Being able to say you 'work at the university' (even one hour a week moving furniture) gives you instant status, catapulting you from social class E (unemployed homeless non-person) to A (alpha-grade graduate employed in education sector). When working on securing that all-important flat, you can mention that you 'have to get back to the lab' even if all you are doing is washing the test tubes. The fact that in your 'spare time' you are working in rocket science will cut no ice with a prospective landlord who does not know or care about your labour of love nor want any share in the financial house of cards by which you propose to fund it.

Getting a job in the university – especially in your own department – can also be a way of getting the foot in the door – literally. If for some reason your PhD registration expires, or you are left in some bureaucratic limbo, which means that you are no longer technically a student (which means no student card, travel discounts, etc) it can be very handy to have your university staff card to let you in the building out of hours, and to use the computer that your status as a researcher (even a part-time one) affords you.

And of course getting a job in some way related to your academic discipline is even better (see next chapter).

7
Academia

While doing your PhD, you have a great opportunity to get into the swing of the wider academic life: the cycle of conferences, funding rounds, journal submissions, lectures, departmental affairs. These experiences can not only be a valuable springboard for your future career – but can also help you directly in pursuit of your doctorate.

Academic research

Academic research is more than peering down a microscope and writing up the results. It needs a context that is supported by disciplinary paradigms, unspoken orthodoxies, peer validation and writing conventions that are nurtured and re-created within a culture of research.

A research culture is one of those things that no self-respecting research-oriented institution can afford to be without. A good research culture is basically a pervasive departmental attitude that research is good: 'we like researchers, and we want to encourage research'. Seminars will be organised and students and staff will turn up and contribute; there will be a social element to the department; probably there will be a generally happy, sociable feel about the place.

A good research culture can and does involve PhD students. It will offer opportunities to participate in the life and work of the department – to the benefit of both.

For a start, you can get a taste for what goes on outside the doctoral cocoon – the realities of fixed-duration projects, teamwork, office politics, the responsibility of delivering results to satisfy someone else's agenda. But, short of taking on a substantial employment commitment, there are still a number of ways of taking first steps towards the full academic job description, which can be fitted in around your thesis commitments, and build up over your doctoral study to a useful portfolio of experience.

Conferences

A conference is more than a good day out, or an excuse to travel. It is one of the basic mechanisms of research discourse and dissemination, where you are expected to contribute and challenge, not just absorb the wisdom dispensed from on high.

Delivering a conference paper is a good way of forcing yourself to write something – a contained mini 'thesis', in effect – to a fixed deadline; it forces you to get to the point, to scratch your head and think if you are really saying something worthwhile. As a PhD student, it is not as if you will be the only researcher doing this – professors of many years' standing also use conference papers to float ideas, and set out preliminary research frameworks, as much as presenting finished results or breakthroughs.

A conference is a great chance to risk testing out some of your ideas with other people. If you ever felt misunderstood and stifled back in your own department, now is the chance to be misunderstood and exposed abroad. Conferences are good occasions to make new contacts and – after a few years have slipped past – renew old acquaintances. Look out for conferences that interest you, but also ask your supervisor, since he or she is likely to know which are the best environments to first expose your developing thesis. They may even suggest writing a joint paper, which may be a useful collaborative experience in its own right (see also Chapter 11, Rehearsing your defence).

Book reviews

Another way to make a start in academic production is to write book reviews for journals. This can be a useful exercise, since you get to read books hot off the press, you get to learn the character of the different journals – useful later when it comes to tailoring papers for publication. Knowing that your review will be fixed in print and distributed around the world rather than just being another 'take' on your thesis, read only by your supervisor, will sharpen your critical capacity: what you are really saying, to what end.

You don't need to be the world's greatest expert in a topic to provide fair criticism of a book. However, bear in mind that it is easier to point out faults in a book (just as in a thesis) than to offer constructive appreciation. Anyone can spot a diagram printed upside down; to mention only this but miss the bigger intellectual picture could look petty. Look out or ask around for journals that invite book reviewers. Getting into the habit of writing reviews gets you into the habit of writing to order, which can stand you in good stead when it comes to tackling 'the big one'. In writing a book review, you may even develop a point that you later use in the thesis itself.

Lab demonstrations

Instructing undergraduates in how to carry out experiments is something of a rite of passage for many PhD students in the life sciences. Besides being a good way of earning money, it is also valuable teaching experience. And since it is a timetabled activity, you can build it in to your weekly routine without it being destructive.

Lecturing and tutoring

It is not unknown for PhD students to be called upon to give lectures. The question of whether you are being used as cheap labour or being given valuable work experience is a vexed one that we shall not address here. However, it is quite time-consuming, since you will have to prepare the lecture notes, overheads and so forth in advance, as well as actually giving the lecture and marking any assignments. You might find, in the end, that you are more willing to forego the money than spend the time and effort required to do a good job.

Giving tutorials is different. It is still time-consuming, although less so than lecturing. And because tutorials tend to be more discursive, they can be far more rewarding. And since you do not have to prepare presentations, they are also less time-consuming than lectures.

Being a supervisor

Being a supervisor is a noble calling; however, it is not normally expected of those in mid pursuit of their *own* PhD. Yet, as a PhD student you may find other PhD students coming to you for advice, not only of a general kind (how do you do a literature review?) but looking for specific and even substantial feedback on their own thesis or research programme. Feedback and student-to-student support are both very important and admirable; but shaping someone else's research project is another matter. If any substantial guidance is being sought, it may be a symptom that the student is not being supervised properly, and is dangerously adrift. Consider if that person's supervisor would appreciate your involvement, or if you could be expected to take any credit for it. You would do well to avoid being dragged into the role of surrogate supervisor – at least until you have got your own PhD out the way.

Marking

Marking student assignments and exam scripts is a good way of getting into a critical mode, assessing what is good and bad. Even if only engaged for the shortest period, the experience of being on the other side can bring valuable insights on what it is to judge and be judged – as one who yourself will eventually be submitting for examination. After exposure to a few offerings, you can quickly start to see how the good start differentiating themselves from the bad; how clear definition and aims of an assignment can ensure a clear direction and argument; the extent to which poor referencing or presentation can spoil otherwise sound research, but on the other hand, how no amount of meticulous formatting or presentation can rescue a bad piece of academic work.

Invigilation

Normally dreadfully dull, and contributing nothing to your thesis. Except for helping fund – or recover from – your extra-curricular lifestyle. For example, it's a benign occupation if you are recovering from a late night: it's warm, quiet, and you don't have to think. Just make sure you turn up, and *don't ever fall asleep*.

Research employment

If you have shown aptitude and reliability you may get a full-time research post, and who knows, maybe even a foot on the ladder towards becoming a fully tenured member of the academic staff.

Getting a job working for your supervisor can be beneficial – though this can be a double-edged sword. On the plus side, if your supervisor becomes your boss, this gives you the right to bang on their door at any time demanding an audience (it is their project, after all, that you are doing the work on). Rather than tiptoeing around the department, putting off seeing them (as your supervisor) because you haven't written that promised chapter, you have an excuse to talk to them about something else, and the channels of communication may be improved. And if the work is in roughly the same area as your PhD topic, you may save time and money by being paid to read dull journals and attend conferences that you would have to have done anyway. And, in principle, you should be able to excuse your PhD work being late because you were working on your job (or vice versa).

In practice, your boss/supervisor might not be so accommodating. In general, having your supervisor as a boss rather puts all your eggs in the one basket. If the going is good, you may flourish. But if relations should break down, both props to your career could implode simultaneously, and then to whom do you turn? It is easier to sound off about your boss to your supervisor (or vice versa) if they are not the same person.

Ludwig Wittgenstein

The story of Wittgenstein's doctorate is a rather long and complex one, but since this seems to fit the spirit of the PhD experience, it bears retelling.

Having originally studied engineering and natural sciences, Wittgenstein embarked on doctoral research in engineering at the University of Manchester in 1908. He first studied the aerodynamics of kites in the upper atmosphere, and then moved on to aeronautical research, successfully designing and testing a novel kind of propeller. A neat piece of practical engineering: so far so good.

However, he felt he needed to know more mathematics, and headed off to Cambridge University to study under Bertrand

Russell, in 1912. Russell was impressed by his talent for mathematical philosophy, and persuaded him to stay on at Cambridge, rather than complete his engineering work at Manchester. Wittgenstein obliged, but in due course, in pursuit of his theoretical research, he headed off for a remote mountain cabin in Norway, where he developed some of his fundamental ideas on the foundations of mathematical logic, that would later form what was to become his PhD thesis.

Then the Great War intervened, and Wittgenstein went off to join the Austrian army. Still, he continued with his philosophical work, working on his notebooks in the trenches; and once taken captive, completed in an Italian prison camp a draft manuscript for the *Tractatus Logico-Philosophicus*, which was to become one of the most influential philosophy books of the twentieth century. The *Tractatus* was published in 1921 – Wittgenstein's only major work published in his lifetime.

Wittgenstein considered that he had now solved the problem of philosophy, and returned to Austria, where he worked variously as a primary school teacher and a gardener's assistant in a monastery.

In the meantime, his work had brought him some fame in the world of philosophy, and eventually he was attracted back to Cambridge in 1929. However, he could not assume an academic post at Cambridge, having never actually completed a degree. He faced having to apply as an undergraduate; but Russell reckoned that his *Tractatus*, combined with his previous residency at Cambridge, would allow him to qualify for a doctoral degree. The *Tractatus* was duly examined by Russell and G. E. Moore. In his examiner's report, Moore is supposed to have noted: 'In my opinion this is a work of genius; it is, in any case, up to the standards of a degree from Cambridge.'

And so, over 20 years after first having embarked on a PhD in engineering, Wittgenstein emerged with his first degree, a Doctorate in Philosophy.

8
Thesis Construction

'The composition of vast books is a laborious and impoverishing extravagance. To go on for five hundred pages developing an idea whose perfect oral exposition is possible in a few minutes! A better course of procedure is to pretend that these books already exist, and then to offer a résumé, a commentary.' Prologue to 'Fictions', Jorge Luis Borges

Writing up is, for many PhD students, a long, hard slog. For the unlucky majority who do not enjoy, or who even fear writing, it is something to be delayed, dreaded and avoided if at all humanly possible. The problem is that – unlike Borges' wishful commentary – you have to do it – the whole thesis and nothing but the thesis; the question is how to make it less painful.

The big one

Your thesis may well be the longest thing that you – or anyone you know who is not doing a PhD – will ever write. But it is not the length, the sheer volume, that is the hard bit. After all, this amount of words is spread out over several years. Your friends in normal occupations may easily write as many words, if not more, in the same period. So it is not the volume of words that counts, as such. It is the sustained length of a single argument that is impressive. It is like taking the amount of words you would say in a week, and making them into a single day-long speech, that is original, without any repetition or inconsistency.

Overall, it is quite likely that your thesis has fewer words than the overall output of your friends in business or other occupations. Because, over the time that you spend on your PhD, the majority of *their* written words are indeed 'final output': but they are text set free as emails, letters and reports – a far more fragmentary collection than the cohesive narrative that is your thesis.

On the other hand, think of the proportion of the words you write over all those years that never see the light of day. All those drafts and re-drafts, all those out-takes, incomprehensible tangents, abandoned chapters, truncated digressions, spiked footnotes. It is quite likely that you write more words that are never part of any finished product than ever go into your thesis. So it is quite likely that if you piled up all the written outputs of your business pals, they would stack up to a much bigger, rangier spiel than your thesis. The thesis is then cast not as a huge lumbering behemoth, but a highly condensed nugget of quality material: no longer and no shorter than absolutely necessary.

What the thesis is

The thesis (or dissertation – the two are used interchangeably) serves two purposes. The first is to demonstrate that you know how to do research. The second, which follows from the first, is to set out a record of your research: why and how you did it, and the implications of your findings.

In these respects, it is akin to an examination script, and the viva voce is the examination in which you defend your thesis. So although you will not find it in any of the rule books, there is an orthodox structure to a thesis and it goes (something) like this:

■ introduction

■ literature review

■ methodology

■ findings

■ discussion

■ conclusion.

This is also the standard structure for articles in academic journals, so there is something to be said for staying with the orthodox approach, both in terms of learning how to work within this framework, and in terms of making life easier for yourself. There is nothing stopping you from breaking with the orthodoxy, but you had better have good reason for doing so: such an obvious deviation from the norm invites close scrutiny from the examiners.

Narrative structure

A thesis is not a novel: the reader does not expect dramatic revelations halfway through or twists in the tail at the end. A good old maxim that works for a PhD thesis is 'say what you are going to say, say it, say what you've just said.' This means that any dramatic revelations should be clearly anticipated in the introduction, and just as clearly claimed credit for at the end.

Thesis components

These are the main components of a thesis, and are typically all included in the word count. Footnotes and appendices are usually *not* counted: take care to check the rules on this anyway.

Title

The length, style and specificity of a thesis title can tell us a little of what a thesis might actually be about. You may go for a grandiloquent title, a concisely coded title with knowing wordplay, a systematic one that will locate your work precisely within the grand scheme of the research structure of the universe; something idiosyncratic, obscure or downright opaque. If it is too specific, it may only be accessed by a few people; if too general, it may not be considered worth looking at by the kind of people who would be looking up PhD theses. As ever, there is no right or wrong way – but do be guided by precedent in your discipline. Consider the merits of standing out from the crowd, or the benefits of saying plainly 'what it says on the tin'. Pragmatically speaking, the shorter the title, the more likely it could be confused with something else (especially in internet searches); the longer the title, the more likely you are to mis-spell or forget it!

Examples of PhD titles

Genetic analyses of albatrosses: mating systems, population structure and taxonomy

The gendered language of Protestant anti-papist polemic in England, 1603-1702

The crystallographic analysis of the *Bacillus thuringiensis* δ-endotoxin Cry1Ac, on its own and in a complex with its receptor ligand, N-acetylgalactosamine

Cross-examination: a critical examination

The politics of reception: Richard Wagner's Die Meistersinger von Nurnburg in Weimar Germany

Assessing motivational strength and studies of boredom and enrichment in pigs

From factories to fine art: the origins and evolution of East London's artists' agglomeration 1968–98

The Pre-history of Post-modernity: Victor Gruen and the Shopping Mall

Abstract

This is the bit that will appear in library searches, and will also be the first section that the examiner reads. That means that it is worth getting it right. The abstract should give an overview of what the project set out to understand; the context of the project; why, and then how the project was carried out; and what the findings of the project were. In other words, it is a one-page summary of your PhD.

Introduction

This chapter should map out what lies ahead, set out clearly the scope and objectives (very important since this could be what you are judged on) and it should be in keeping with what you actually do in the rest of the thesis. It should be neither over- nor under-ambitious; it may also encompass the whole thesis including main findings, so that there are no surprises. After reading your introduction, the examiner should be inspired to read on, yet relaxed in knowing the finite territory to be covered and the general destination.

Literature review

Here you are demonstrating that your project has not been done before, and that it needs doing. This chapter should therefore set out the general context, and then focus in on the issue at hand, by trying to offer an even-handed summary of the research, highlighting any contradictions, significant breakthroughs, and finally, any gaps in the research that need plugging – this is the justification for your own research (see also Searching the literature, in Chapter 5).

Methodology

This should set out a detailed account of how you did the research, and will probably include details of pilot studies (ie a mini-project to test the methodology). It is not unknown for the methodology chapter to be rewritten in the light of how the research was actually done, as opposed to how it was intended. It is also not unknown for the rationale for the methodology to be articulated only *after* the research has been carried out – clearly not good research practice, but perhaps not so surprising in light of the iterative nature of much research (see also Methodology: research as an iterative process, in Chapter 5).

Findings

This chapter will take the reader (ie the examiner) through the findings of your research, tying them back into the existing literature, and highlighting the more significant outcomes that you will explore in greater length in the next chapter.

Discussion

This chapter is in effect a continuation of the previous one, but shifts from exploring the findings to explaining and analysing them. Here, you should be offering your own insights as to the way in which your own research advances knowledge within your field, and how and why that is the case.

Conclusion

On reaching the conclusion, the examiner should already be reasonably satisfied that you have done enough to pass. The conclusion should therefore flag up innovative points, tick off things you said you would do in the introduction, synthesise threads across chapters, demonstrate that you know the significance of what you have found, and, lastly, make suggestions for further research (which shows the value of your own contribution).

Incidentally, do not try to introduce new material here: if it merits inclusion in the thesis, it should be in the main body of the work. If there are any rabbits to be pulled out of hats, the apparatus and methodology for doing so should have been set out long before now. If new points do arise in the conclusion, these could be expressed as areas for further research.

References

References are a necessary part of academic work, and a task to be started early on in the process, particularly if you intend to use bibliographic software. References are *always* checked assiduously by examiners, so it is worth getting them right.

The most efficient referencing system for PhD purposes is the Harvard system, whereby the reference – author, year, page number – is put in brackets within the text: thus (Marshall & Green, 2004, p.23). An alphabetical list of references (by author) is included at the end of the thesis. Each reference lists the author(s), date of publication, title, place of publication and publisher. So:

Marshall, S. & Green, N., 2004, *Your PhD Companion*, Oxford, How To Books.

The point is that the examiner should be able to see immediately what the references are – footnotes and endnotes are a nuisance in this respect – and the examiner should also be able to track down the work referenced quickly and easily, should they so choose. Lastly, this is the system favoured by most academic journals, so while it may not be the most graphically elegant solution, it is by far the most useful for PhD purposes.

Appendices

Appendices are an optional extra to be inserted after the references, and not usually included in the word count. Here you can include supplementary material, detailed charts and other research findings, translations of foreign language quotations and so forth.

Footnotes

Some people hate footnotes, thinking of them as nothing more than annoying distractions; for others judicious use of them can help improve the overall flow of the main text, by locating additional facts or explanation off-line. The information in footnotes is particularly useful if elaborating on a point or anticipating some counter-argument that might occur to the reader, but which you don't want to treat in full. However, you wish to show you are aware of it, so that the reader is not ploughing on for pages with the nagging thought that you have missed something or are still to address it.

Footnotes can also be used liberally during thesis construction, even if there is a final cull at the end to ensure readability. Footnotes can be temporary 'holding areas' that exchange what's in with what's out. What starts life as a curious aside that is given a berth as a footnote may turn out to become an important new angle in the main text. Conversely, what was once a solid paragraph might be shunted into a footnote for the time being, and end up dropping out altogether, as the flow of the main thesis shifts its course above.

Literature revisited

Compiling a bibliography can be a grinding chore if you did not take proper notes of references – if you only ever scribbled down the author and title, but forgot the volume or page number – when you were eagerly devouring the literature in your first year. While it is easy to look up an electronic database to check the things like subtitles, or date and place of publication (which you may have forgotten to do first time around) it may be hard or impossible to track down things like page numbers of particular quotations without revisiting the source. This may seem small beer for any individual case, but the cumulative amount of revisiting can amount to a substantial library marathon at the end of your writing up period, which you may not have budgeted for. Still, revisiting in your final year references you maybe skimmed over casually in your first year may spark off some new insights that could add creatively to the final work.

Bibliographic by-ways

The anoraks among us can take solace or amusement by formulating bibliographic statistics as we go along: like a league table of cities in which references were published; most popular cited authors (ranking your supervisors and other colleagues); median date of publication; and last but not least, seeing if you can get all letters in the alphabet represented (Aaron to Zubay). These pastimes are almost completely unnecessary, but can at least help keep one's sense of curiosity awake, in what could otherwise be a very dull task. At the most, it can alert you to deficiencies in the reference list (too out of date, too Anglophone, and so on). Most likely, it is simply a bit of fun to keep spirits up between jaded PhD students.

Language and writing style

What style: safe and dry or racy and dangerous? The aim of academic writing is to present a dispassionate, unambiguous account that relies on facts and carefully shaped argument, and for this reason usually makes for pretty dry reading. 'Racy' by academic standards can still be turgid by journalistic or novelistic standards, and striking a balance between rigour, clarity and eloquence is no easy matter.

It is possible though, and something to be aimed for. Of course you will find your own style as you go through the writing process, and you will probably find that as you become more comfortable your style changes for the better. As a consequence, you might decide to rewrite some of your – perfectly acceptable – older work for purely stylistic reasons.

Writing style will also be dictated by your discipline, and your background in that discipline. An urban history will read very differently from a technical account of lab work, or from a tract on the philosophical underpinnings of a great novelist: there will be rubriks to follow, more or less firmly laid down by your supervisors and the likely expectations of your examiners.

Above all though, and no matter what your discipline, you should aim for clarity of expression. A dry thesis that makes sense will get the message across, and that, in the end, is what matters.

Writing in English as a foreign language

As native English language speakers, we can only say that we are impressed by anyone who not only completes a PhD, but does so in a second language. The bottom line is that it is hard work, but here are some pointers from people who have done it, to help you to know what to expect.

- You may have to develop a new style to suit the language. For example, someone who writes concisely in Spanish (which when written is expansive) might find that the same approach yields a very abrupt style in English (which tends to innate compactness), requiring them to adopt the opposite style.

- Your vocabulary will be smaller, so you will find expressing yourself precisely will be difficult.

- You will not be able to write as quickly.

Overall (and there are exceptions to this) if you are writing in a foreign language you should expect to make more effort to produce something with which you are less satisfied, compared to your native language. Your university may offer courses on thesis writing, and these can prove useful, so you should try to find out about them. Buy a good English dictionary, a good (your language)-English dictionary, a guide to English grammar, and (importantly) a thesaurus.

Finally, you should try to write every day. Practice, as they say, makes perfect, and the more you have written before the critical writing-up period, the less you will be worrying about your English when you get there.

Holding a whole thesis in your head

As your thesis builds up, you normally only have to hold a few sections or chapters in mind simultaneously, or an outline of the whole thesis at a low resolution. But sooner or later – especially towards the end – you may have to load up the whole thing into your brain, to be able to 'see' it all simultaneously, to mentally navigate from end to end, to visualise individual words and images, to make links, and weed out inconsistencies, to grasp and forge the whole thesis. It can be like trying to imagine the national atlas of a country and all the local maps and street maps of all the cities and towns at the one time. To do this can require a lot of concentration, and a decent chunk of undisturbed time, to immerse yourself sufficiently to allow instant visualisation, navigation, synthesis and harmonisation.

Writing processes

Writer's block

What can we say about it? Er… Awful if you get it. Try writing anything – random gibberish; or scribble why you can't say what you want to – just to get you writing something, and then steer the flow back to the thread of your thesis. If the writing really is hopeless, try doing other things for a while: getting your bibliography up to date, standardising your diagrams, reading the rules for thesis format, or doing research on your prospective examiners. These things have to be done sooner or later, but in doing them now, they may even spark a train of thought that gets you writing again.

From pieces to thesis

If you think of writing up as a gradual process rather than a single act, it immediately becomes more tractable a problem. If you try to write your thesis from scratch in the space of three months, you will quickly drive yourself mad, so don't do it. Instead, start writing as soon as you can (the literature review and methodology chapters can be started relatively early, for example), and work at it steadily, chipping away over the period of a year or more, a bit here, a bit there, so that gradually you accumulate a pile of paper that contains most of what you want and need to say.

It might sound flippant, but simply generating the volume of work matters, not because that's what the rules require, but because it gives you a sense of being able to do it, of being in control. And that is hugely important to your progress. Even if this pile of paper – in effect your first draft – needs considerable editing, and probably it will, you have at least reached that milestone. You can move from a process of writing to a process of editing. To be sure, you might well end up rewriting large chunks of your work, deleting entire sections, and writing new sections. You will be restructuring the work on a massive level, combining parts here to create a new chapter, and splitting chapters elsewhere to make them more accessible to the reader.

Structuring

Sometimes you may find you have hashed and rehashed and the bits just don't fit. Or you are struggling with a completely straggling network of ideas, that don't easily fit a narrative thread. One way is to cut it up into smaller chunks, and then just introduce a list of points, in no particular order. Once you start writing the chunks, an order might suggest itself. Or, you could write down all the subsections on pieces of paper or card, and then shuffle them around to try to get an order. Sometimes the structural problem runs deeper, and you may just need to leave it to the side. At some point, you might get a new inspiration or sudden new perspective which suggests a new order that everything can then be fitted into.

Frankenstein's thesis

Editing a draft thesis can be like performing surgery on Dr Frankenstein's monster. Laid bare in front of you, you see it in all its imperfection. You see how lumpy and ugly it is, how dysfunctional. You can still see all the scars – and the bolts are clearly visible. But Frankenstein did not set out to create a monster; he meant to create a new person. So it needs some surgery.

But it needs more than cosmetic surgery to get it right. There is no point in simply stretching some skin over the bolts and sewing it up. It needs some major, deeper surgery. The patient also needs to be cut down in size, yet it is still incomplete. It still needs some parts removed for some other experiment, and new ones added. But it is a messy job. Will it all fit back in? Will it come out better than it was before? And will all those disparate parts, so long kept in drawers and pickle jars, work when they are put together, to make a whole? Do they really belong in this body, or would it be better to form them into a less ambitious creation? The question dreaded by the surgeon: 'When will you finish?' cuts deeper for the monster: 'Will you ever be finished?'

Unwriting

The desperation of not writing enough may generate such a momentum that it carries you well over the thesis word limit. You then switch from writing to unwriting. Where before you measured progress by obsessively hitting the wordcount function on your wordprocessor, watching the words mount up, you now carefully take note as words are whittled away again. Less becomes more.

This stage can at least be satisfying as you have overcome the angst of under-delivery and writer's block; having seen the maximum extent of your thesis's expression, you have become surer of what the main points are, and can take satisfaction from noting as rangy text gets tightened up, complicated passages simplified, red herrings and blind alleys are purged. Altogether you fondly hope your long-suffering examiner will appreciate the efforts, as if they will be grateful to face only 99,999 words.

The obese thesis

With an obese thesis, the more of it there is, the more the effort and energy will be needed just to keep it all hanging together: the more time required to edit each iteration, the more errors there will be needing correction, the more pages and ink cartridges you will use up and wear out each time you want a physical copy of it. So, unless you positively revel in your glorious bulk, it's best to 'lean up' if you can – not least for the benefit of the reader.

Dr Seuss

'Dr Seuss', author and cartoonist of *The Cat in the Hat* fame, was the pen-name of Theodor Seuss Geisel. He actually set out to do a PhD in literature, at Oxford University (where, at least, he found himself a wife). However, he dropped out after deciding that his studies were 'astonishingly irrelevant', and turned instead to the serious business of creating characters such as the Fractious Sneetches, Zubble-wumps and the Ooey-gooey Green Ooblecks. Geisel maybe never wrote a PhD thesis, but in the end perhaps made more out of less. In 1960, for a bet, he succeeded in writing an entire book using only 50 words. The book, *Green Eggs and Ham*, became one of the best-selling children's books of all time.

9
Survival

In the late stages of your PhD, the processes of writing up your thesis and life as a PhD student can become entangled in a single struggle for survival. This chapter explores this twilight zone, which can be the toughest stage of doing a PhD.

Climbing at altitude

You may have sailed though your education up until now; doing a PhD might then seem the next obvious step, and the final pinnacle of your education. But in many respects doing a PhD is not just a higher level pursuit, but a whole new game. The skills and qualities that got you where you are now are not necessarily sufficient to get you through your doctorate.

It is as if you have been doing some mountaineering, and consider yourself quite experienced and successful. You are. Up to a point. But then, you hit altitude, you hit ice, a blizzard comes down, the air thins. The rules of survival are different. Being good at climbing – as such – may no longer be enough.

An expedition up here requires competence in a new medium. Your successful mission is as much to do with logistics of estimating distances and times, rationing your food, taking care about altitude sickness and frostbite, as it is to do with 'climbing'.

This might be a bit of a shock, if you have been used to striding through the foothills and minor peaks of your education up until now. Now, for the first time, you might experience self-doubt. You might look around the freezing wasteland of your doctorate, an icefield in the middle of nowhere, and wonder what you are doing here. Where are the panoramic ridges that inspired you to take up mountaineering in the first place? Is this what you really want?

Before, there was always a challenge ready set out for you – a cliff-face to shin up, a ridge to traverse, or a pinnacle set out ready for you to scale – as if the whole educational geology was set out for you to find and conquer. But here, the topographical acrobatics seem to have petered out; you seem to have come out on to some sort of lonely plateau, where you have to conjure up your own summit before being able to scale it.

So it's a different kind of challenge, with a leaner kind of reward: where just being here, breathing and surviving this long, feels like an achievement. At times your motivation to do the PhD has nothing to cling to except the most abstract, last-resort rationale of the mountaineer: 'because it's there'.

PhD completion and attrition

Not all who set out to do a PhD end up getting one. It is not unusual to find that half of those who embark on a PhD fail to finish. PhD completion rates vary from country to country, from university to university, and from subject to subject.

In general, natural and life sciences tend to have higher completion rates than arts and humanities. Reasons include more external grant funding, more cohesive and competitive research environments, and more frequent contact between students and supervisors. Perhaps successful completion is also connected to the way that science PhD students are often following a clearly targeted or 'convergent' research path, rather than a more exploratory or 'divergent' research exploration with arts subjects. It could also be that in some kinds of objective discipline, a certain amount of clearly articulated quantified material may be relatively easily adjudged to be 'enough', whereas in more subjective fields, one may never be sure when enough is enough, leading to a more open-ended investigation that – while clearly capable of being drawn to a successful conclusion – may run the risk of losing its way and being 'never finished'.

Completion rates (and time taken to completion) have been widely recognised as relating directly to the quality of the graduate education experience. Factors such as a sense of belonging, peer group support and treatment as full members of the academic community have been attributed to the successful PhD experience, as much as good supervision and adequate funding.

In a survey of PhD students in New Zealand, every interviwee remarked on 'the sense of isolation and lack of social contact' experienced during the PhD process, and it would be fair to say that this circumstance alone can make writing up seem like one painful step too many.

Indeed, a recent report refers to the 'painfully slow attrition of the all-but-dissertation (ABD) students that occurs years after all other program requirements are successfully completed' – in other words, students who clearly could and should be expected to finish, but for one reason or another fail to do so. They may find a job that neither requires the PhD (even if it requires the knowledge gathered along the way) nor leaves time for its successful completion. If they hate writing and their ambitions lie outside the world of academia, they may just decide that they've had enough, and simply stop coming into the office. What all this means is that at some point, probably towards the end, you will find that your enthusiasm is all but exhausted, as are your patience and bank account. At this point you will find out just how determined you are, because at this stage, it's not fun any more: you are writing on will-power alone (see also Wanting to do a PhD; Who to do it with?, in Chapter 2).

Mission to Mars

Doing a PhD is like going on a mission to Mars. You blast off to a great fanfare; your friends and family cheer you on with good wishes. They watch you disappear off into the sky – secretly thinking you might be rather brave, if not crazy, to do it – and turn their attention back to Earth. You have become just some faraway object who either (a) has got to Mars or (b) hasn't.

The PhD is a long, exhausting journey, and though you may have to convince yourself it's heroic – just to get you through – the reality can sometimes be rather dull and isolating. Part of the problem is that there are precious few tangible milestones for anyone outside the process to relate to. On the one hand, the big things are too obvious, too few and far between. Sure, so you can see the Moon from there; right, now what about Mars?

On the other hand, the small things are too obscure, dull and routine to be of interest to anyone else. You may be in rarefied territory, but what did you actually do today? Did some experiments; stared into space; wrote up the log; had a packet meal of soya-protein for dinner; gave up on the idea of a sex life for another year. Ah look, over there, another star. No one but you can really grasp the daily inching forward of your mission; everyone else just wants to know when you get there.

And when you do occasionally see something amazing – a new multi-coloured moon that no one suspected had ever existed, or the view back to your homeland picked out in an oblique moon-beam shadow, you find it very difficult to explain the new insights you have found, or properly share the excitement of an extraordinary new perspective.

Losing your bearings

In general, your whole worldview has become somewhat remote, and you may find it increasingly difficult to relate to what was normal life back in what used to pass for the real world. What seemed normal becomes completely transformed. You lose your bearings, then find new ones, that gradually drift away from normal terrestrial ones. It may seem normal to you now to get up when it is dark, and work for ten hours, and then go to sleep when the sun comes up (or goes down).

The people back home who have not done a PhD just cannot relate to you because they haven't been there. Those who have been there – the old pro astronauts safely back home – may have been there, but they lack an immediate sense of sympathy, since after all, they've been through hell and back – and got over it. In fact, they may be blanking out the horror of it all – the fearful vastness, the bleak insecurity, the dark thoughts of no return …and balk at the thought of going back to accompany you.

So, you start losing track, losing touch with anyone not actually doing a PhD. They don't want to hear any more about your latest multi-coloured moon: just when you actually get to Mars. And you don't want to hear about their normal lives, material advancement, weekends at leisure – or what's on at the cinema or anything in the news or anywhere. Your interest in all these superfluous things – things that do not help you get there – was thrown overboard a long time ago.

So messages home become fewer and further between. Responses get more and more delayed. The line becomes crackled and tense, with many pauses. Your conversational skills atrophy, and you start avoiding talking to save energy.

As you get deeper into this alien lifestyle, the only people you may really be able to relate to are the other space-mates on board, whose position you can understand deeply – perhaps too closely. If you are lucky, you may form mutually supportive friendships. If you are unlucky, you may end up with a desperate catfight for control of your capsule – your fragile niche of doctoral survival – a petty battle for paper, toner and coffee whitener.

In the end, your doctoral journey may have changed you – as much as your undergraduate one ever did. When you look back at Earth, you might see a different planet. You may have become so acclimatised to your capsule life that you may just stay there.

Plotting your course in PhD-space

If doing a PhD is like going to Mars, then plotting your course to get there is a similarly challenging task – somewhere between management studies and rocket science.

The first problem is that you start out with a flat-Earth, or pre-Copernican view of the universe. From normal grounded reality, the PhD trajectory looks quite straightforward. You surely just blast off for the Moon (which is, after all, 'just up there'), turn left (avoiding the sun), go a bit further, and you get to Mars. So, if Mars is your final thesis, the Moon is your upgrade report; a handy springboard, once you have got there, just keep going for another few years and you're there. Simple?

But once you are cast loose from your territorial grounding, away from the daily rhythms of normal life, the bounds of the world of work, even the relative certainties of taught courses with their regular cycles of classes, exams and resits, you find yourself in a changed new landscape. You are no longer fixed down to anything; you are not even sure what is up or down any more. Out here, everything is moving about; the PhD has become a moving target, a cunning, swerving, coruscating beast, and where you set out from is no longer quite the terra firma you once thought it was.

Another problem is that you find a whole series of tempting new planets all swinging around in different orbits, like new projects and creative enterprises, research networks, university politics, jobs. Often, these start out looking like stepping stones, helping you plot your course towards Mars, or build up momentum to swing beyond it once you get there. But soon they may appear as distractions, competing targets, taking you in completely different directions.

You begin to realise that your ultimate destination now looks further away than it did from the ground. Mars is maybe now a receding red dot, on the other side of the sun, in an entirely different direction from where it was when you originally aimed at it. You get the feeling that to get there now, you shouldn't be starting from here.

A real problem is that this complicated trajectory you are careering around on makes absolutely no sense to those back home. If you do take an interesting detour round Venus, or a daring short-cut past the sun, you are in danger of confusing those who thought they were supporting a trip to Mars in the other direction entirely. Or you lose yourself in the asteroid belt, making a series of fascinating discoveries that would be 'whole PhD topics in their own right' if only you had time to write them up. They might even be more interesting than going all the way to Mars, but no one has heard of your new asteroids, and you know you won't get any peace until you get to Mars.

If you finally get there, you may find that your voyage of exploration was much richer than you had imagined to make up for the much longer time it took you to do it. But hopefully it will have been worth it. In that case, you may be glad that your original simple model of the universe was sufficiently undaunting to tempt you off the ground in the first place.

Working and writing up

Rare is the PhD student who writes up their thesis, submits it, takes a holiday between submission and viva, makes any necessary corrections, hands in the completed PhD thesis, has the weekend off and starts work on the Monday. Very rare.

What normally happens is this, or something like it. Towards the end of your funded period, you will start wondering what to do next. This has no connection with your PhD progress. You will also start worrying about income generally. This, too, has no connection with your PhD progress. You may well get offered consultancy work, or a post-doc position by your supervisor. Again, this has no connection with your PhD progress.

If the money is short, and for most people at this stage it is, you will accept the position. This has *everything* to do with your PhD progress. Depending on how disciplined you are, your PhD will be shifted onto the back burner, and it will cease to be a part of your everyday life. Instead, it will be something to be done at weekends and in the evenings after work. It will be something that stops you from going out, and makes you guiltily grumpy when you do. It becomes something you would really rather not think about.

There is no real way around this. Disliking your job helps, because you can then treat writing up as a hobby, but that assumes that you don't hate writing up. If you can arrange to work flexible hours and have a computer at home, you can work on your thesis in the morning (when you are fresh) and make up the time by working on your 'day job' into the evening. That at least has the advantage that you don't have to start all over again once you get home from work, probably tired and hungry. You could also try to arrange to work a four-day week, leaving yourself a clear weekday to do the PhD, but again, this assumes a sympathetic employer. Even then it can prove difficult in practice if you are needed at work on your 'PhD day'.

'Difficult in practice' is perhaps the phrase to remember from this section: it's certainly do-able, but it is hard work.

Unravelling purposes

It is when the going gets tough that the sturdiness of your objectives may get most called into question. If your main reason for doing a PhD was simply to get someone to finance your student lifestyle for three more years, then having done that, the struggle to write up may pall if you are being offered some more immediately career-fulfilling occupation elsewhere. Similarly, if your objective was largely to do a certain piece of research, then you might be tempted to go straight out and apply it, rather than go through the motions of getting an academic degree. We know of one talented PhD student who was so successful in (and satisfied by) publishing his ongoing research before he started writing up formally, that the effort of actually shaping the material into a thesis became an insurmountable looking prospect.

Unfinished business

Alan Greenspan studied for a PhD in economics at Columbia until he ran out of money. He went into business, and later became Chairman of the US Federal Reserve Bank.

Folk-rock singer-songwriter Art Garfunkel started on a PhD in mathematics but gave it up for a musical career.

Brian May started a PhD in astronomy, but was diverted by the global fame of being guitarist with the rock group Queen. He later was awarded an Honorary Doctorate.

Magnum opus

One good piece of advice you may hear from time to time is that a PhD is an exercise in research training, and your thesis should not be regarded as your 'magnum opus' – or a repository of all your life's work. Certainly, the thesis may well be the biggest single piece of work you will have done, before or since; and it is likely to represent the greatest expression of your knowledge and development of ideas at the time.

'At the time' gets to the heart of the matter. Your research, intellectual inquiry and life's work are all part of a continuous process, in which your thesis will be just one milestone along the way – albeit a very important one. It may well be the cornerstone of your academic career. But your career has room for lots of milestone works, and it is not essential that all are fitted into your thesis. There is a danger that the 'thesis' – as in academic argument – becomes a rolling programme that is always attempting to be the latest and best exposition of your life's work – a burden that is in danger of never being fulfilled. On the other hand, the 'thesis' as a finite, bound document is more easily seen for what it is, the product of a single programmed piece of research, which may represent the best of your life's work at the time, but which you may already have moved on from by the time you have finished writing it up or by the time you graduate.

Having said this, it is entirely natural to regard your PhD as your life's work. You may be entitled to feel that the thesis (and not the fact of passing the viva) is what is of value: a career-making landmark which demands all the care, attention and time that you can muster. It can feel disconcerting to think one should rein in the work, to deliberately produce something that merely adequately meets examination standard. This is important, because motivation is a key factor of success. Putting it bluntly, doing a PhD may be so difficult, and such a sacrifice at times, that convincing yourself that it is indeed your ultimate 'great work' may be the only way of getting through the pain barrier. In other words, no matter how rationally you might tell yourself that you should regard the thesis as a research training hoop to jump through, emotionally you may need the dream of glorious martyrdom to sustain you.

This, of course, relates back to the idea of why you are doing your PhD, and what you mean to get out of it. If you want your doctoral research to precipitate the realisation of your greatest work – in the process of which you happen to write a piece of text that qualifies you for a PhD – then don't be surprised if the whole process takes significantly longer than a typical doctoral time budget. If on the other hand you simply want to get in, get it done, and get out, and then use the fact of having gained a PhD as the springboard to your life's work, then you will have the satisfaction of facing your great work having already cleared the 'obligation to finish'. Having said that, by the time you finish your career plans may have moved on, and you may find the attractions of having a 'normal life' out of work seem a much better way of passing your days than resurrecting the idea of the magnum opus you already convinced yourself you didn't need to do at the time; the ambition to create the 'ultimate work' may never again be quite such a burning priority as when held hostage by the desperate need to complete an overdue qualification. In a sense it all boils down to the priority afforded to gaining your doctorate, or the value of the thesis as the embodiment of your magnum opus. The choice is yours.

The Devil's bargain

When the going gets tough, your longing to be finished may be so strong that you try to think of any way to escape from your torment. You dream madly of instant release from the burden of your thesis, and the pursuit of your PhD. Late some night, soon enough, the Devil appears with some tempting offers that might just do the trick – at a price...

Devil's bargain no. 1

Upon agreement, you shall be handed instantly a final proof copy of your completed thesis. This shall be the very thesis you had in mind all those years, including all the tantalising nuggets of insight that you found so hard to articulate and write up yourself. The work shall contain and reflect all your best ideas, and all relevant interpolations and extrapolations thereof (if requested, material of equivalent value may be inserted as appropriate). Your thesis will be presented in final examination-ready format – to the correct length, complete with all diagrams, drawn in a consistent style; all citations and footnotes consistently presented and cross-referenced; margins correctly set; pages numbered and printed; and bound in a handsome volume the correct shade of blue. Notwithstanding this advanced state of completion, the Devil and his agents shall arrange for any further edits or amendments that you may require (whether or not in the Devil's opinion these should improve or diminish the quality of the finished product) and shall do so, in principle, for an unlimited number of such edits and amendments, for all eternity. (The Devil does kindly advise, however, that this may defeat the purpose of your entry into this bargain.) The thesis will in any case follow your writing style and tone, such that it will henceforth be seamlessly identifiable with your previous outputs, and form a splendid foundation for your future work. The thesis will be entirely and incontrovertibly yours, and yours to keep. Congratulations! You may now leave university and embark on the rest of your career. The single condition attached is that the thesis is not entered for any doctoral examination. You shall thereby forfeit all rights or claims to completing your PhD forthwith; you shall relinquish your status as PhD candidate (and before you ask, you may not have an MPhil), and abandon any entitlement to use the title 'Doctor' in perpetuity.

Devil's bargain no. 2

Upon agreement, you shall immediately be deemed to have successfully completed, and shall instantly be granted a PhD, and released forthwith from the requirement to submit a thesis for examination. Henceforth you can call yourself Doctor, and are free to leave the building. Your PhD certificate is in the post, with the tickets to your graduation, for all your family and friends. Congratulations! You may resume the rest of your life. There is only one condition. In being released from the requirement to complete your thesis, you shall forfeit the right to all material and intellectual property connected with your doctoral study. The Devil shall retain the thesis – in whatever current state it is in – including all previous drafts and versions thereof, no matter how similar or superfluous, and all other text, graphics and data pertaining to the research, construction and dissemination of the thesis, including all references, citations, footnotes and end-notes. The foregoing shall apply to all media, including all paper hardcopies, notebooks, backs of envelopes and beermats; and all electronic versions, including back-up copies and all detritus from crashed versions of word-processing programs. Every last letter and byte shall be reclaimed (empty disks shall be returned on request). You shall not only cede all rights to the use of this material, but also rescind any claim of association with the research topic itself, or any future appearance of the research in publications such as may be produced from time to time by the Devil's own research associates, who shall in any case enjoy (on behalf of the Devil) all normal rights of ownership in perpetuity.

Dr Johnson

'The greatest part of a writer's time is spent in reading, in order to write; a man will turn over half a library to make one book.' Quoted in Boswell's *Life of Samuel Johnson*.

Samuel Johnson, surely one of the world's most famous 'Doctors', did not do a PhD. In fact, he didn't even have a degree. He did attend Pembroke College, Oxford – where he became 'overwhelmed with an horrible hypochondria ... dejection, gloom, and despair' – but had to drop out due to lack of money. This setback, however, did not stop him pursuing a career in writing, and going on to be one of England's most celebrated scholars, and one of the English language's most quoted authors. As a mark of his accomplishments, he was awarded an honorary doctorate – a Doctor of Laws (LL.D) from Trinity College, Dublin – and his friend Boswell took to calling him 'Dr Johnson'. One of his most famous works was the *Dictionary of the English Language*. Published in 1755, it remained the standard for a century and a half. It took nine years to write and weighed in at two large folio volumes – surely a magnum opus to stave off any thesis envy.

10
The End Game

You have done your research and decided that your thesis (research argument) is worth submitting as a thesis (examinable tome). It is as if you have climbed the mountain, and can now see a great valley open up, with your destination visible in the distance. There is still quite a way to go, and there are still a few final hurdles to get over. Had these been at the start of your journey, they would not have seemed daunting; but towards the end, they may yet be energy sapping. Taking the line of least resistance is now your best strategy.

Entering the end game

Although for most of your time you may feel yourself to be a researcher, or even more generally a scholar, expanding the very frontiers of knowledge, sooner or later you will have to face the fact that you are an examination candidate.

In one university's regulations, PhD candidates are reminded that:

- It is your own decision to submit the thesis in whatever state at whatever time.
- The outcome of the examination is determined by two or more examiners acting jointly.

The effective result is a clear message:

- It is your own fault if you submit an inadequate thesis – not your supervisor's.
- It is no single individual's 'fault' if you receive an adverse result.

This brings home to you that should you decide your newly formed thesis is now worthy of examination, you are now more than ever playing to the rules of a game.

Knowing the rules

The effective competitor will always be aware of the rules of any game – as well as the prizes on offer – before deigning to partake. This goes for the PhD game as much as any other. Knowing the rules is not 'swotty', but downright smart, because it allows you to maximise results for minimum effort. Especially, this can avoid wasting time and effort on the things you cannot easily be judged upon (like just how cool your intellectual heroes are, whom you deftly work into your thesis), but ensures you do not get tripped up on something relatively niggling but definitely punishable (like going a tad over the word limit).

Although when faced with the paperwork it may seem as if there are lots of rules and regulations associated with the award of the PhD degree, the number of rules concerning what is actually required for the submission of a PhD thesis is staggeringly small. What's more, such rules as there are usually refer to things like thickness of paper and how to number your pages. These rules are hardly to do with intellectual prowess, but are typically to do with:

■ Your examiners' eyesight – since the legibility of the document (decent sized lettering on good opaque paper) will help determine whether your examiners will be irritable or not when they come to read your thesis.

■ The thesis office administrators' eyesight and neck muscles, as they strain to locate your 'unique' thesis in a towering pile of other 'unique' theses in the great PhD Hall of Submission, somewhere deep in the admin block of your university.

■ The ease with which your thesis binder can pick up, carry and bind your thesis without wasting *their* time if the pages fall out all over the floor.

University rules will also cover things such as what must be done and by when; details of associated financial penalties if you overrun (a late submission fee, for example); how to embark upon appeals procedures; roughly what is expected of you as a PhD candidate, and roughly what you can expect of your supervisor.

What you will *not* find in the rules is:

■ what is deemed to be 'original' work;

■ what is deemed to be 'sufficient length';

■ what makes a thesis of doctoral standard.

Playing the game

In football there are famously only a few actual rules of the game. While knowing these is necessary, it is not sufficient to be able to play the game in any real sense. The rules tell you what you can and cannot do, but not how to compete and win. Similarly, succeeding at the PhD game is not just about familiarity with the doctoral regulations, but knowing the academic game overall, and in the widest sense, knowing the ways of the world.

In contrast to the business world where success may be measured in narrow commercial terms, or the world of politics where attaining office (rather than changing the world) is the benchmark of success, the PhD might be considered a 'pure' activity, where accomplishment is judged purely in terms of intellectual excellence. However, doing a PhD is still a human activity, and as subject to 'politics' as any other. In any walk of life, merit is awarded through some kind of human agency: those who win national honours, those who get jobs as professors, those who win research grants, those who win Nobel Prizes, are all operating within a system subject to human foibles and prejudices. It is no different with your doctorate: though you may feel you are escaping to an ivory tower, your success there is subject to political forces: what research gets funded, how your topic may be influenced by what the wider discipline demands, what equipment you get hold of, who your supervisors and examiners are.

Therefore, although a successful doctorate will necessarily mean doing a piece of original research – perhaps as 'pure' as any academic research can get – it almost certainly will also require negotiation of the human game that goes on around it. As with other walks of life, a bit of nous and political awareness could help you get further faster than academic ability on its own.

In getting this far, you have done the most remarkable academic part of the doctoral challenge. From here on in, knowing the rules means making sure that your effort is geared towards passing the final examination. The thesis becomes not a magnum opus, but an exam script (see also Choosing your examiners, in Chapter 11, Your relationship with your supervisor, in Chapter 3, and Originality and what it means, in Chapter 5).

Preparing for submission: final content check

Make sure you are ready to submit; make sure you have a clear opinion from your supervisors that it is more or less at examinable state; do a last literature search in case something important has come up recently (especially if you have been 'hibernating' away from the real world for long periods) that would materially affect the integrity of your thesis (there is not necessarily a need to change everything, but you may do well to show awareness of the most recent developments). As with other things, being prepared long in advance is always worthwhile, that is, getting familiar with what a thesis actually is by scrutinising a good selection of previous theses in your field, which you could usefully do from early on in your doctoral study.

Formatting your thesis

The short version goes like this. Read the rules, read the manual, do your homework, give yourself plenty of time.

Here's a longer version for people who want more advice. There are few rules concerning formatting – as ever, check the rules for your institution thoroughly – and those that exist are purely practical, intended to ensure that the thesis is legible and easy to bind accurately. So if you are wondering why your university won't let you print double-sided, it is to make it easier for the binder to get it right (we know because we asked the binder).

Basically though, you need to be thinking practically at this stage. If you want to do something that looks really good, allow yourself time to do so, since graphic design and the like is extremely labour intensive. Think a simple diagram might help explain a tricky concept? Don't try to knock it out in an hour or two, as many do (and then give up), but leave yourself a day. If the concept is that difficult, then expressing it graphically will be time-consuming.

And at the risk of stating the obvious, *do* learn how to use your computer to the full. Read the manuals, use the built-in help – or ask others what they find useful that saves time and effort – it is time well spent. You would be surprised how many people don't bother, and then end up wondering why it takes ages to carry out what would be a simple task if only they knew.

For example, if you learn to use style sheets in a word-processing programme, it will save you time when formatting chapters and preparing a table of contents, since much of the work will be done by the computer. So if you get it right, changing a section title or chapter title will automatically update the table of contents. There is another reason for making an effort to learn your software properly: something that is obviously wrong will demand correction; something that you left out may not be noticed. So make sure it looks good.

■ ■ ■ ■ ▬▬▬▬▬▬▬▬▬▬▬▬▬▬▬▬▬▬▬▬▬▬▬▬▬▬▬

The person who, shortly before they were due to submit, lost their entire thesis when the hard drive in the computer was erased by IT support

Fortunately, the person to whom this happened had a back-up, but it did happen. So keep a back-up. Actually, keep several back-ups. This is one area of doing a PhD where near-total paranoia is a reasonable, even sensible, position to take. Do back up your work onto something reliable, like a CD. More than once.

Acknowledgements

Of all the last minute things you had forgotten to factor in to your 'schedule for completion', the acknowledgements page is likely to be the most satisfying to complete. It is a great chance to cut loose from the burden of scholarship and pre-viva angst, and say a few personal things to the world. But remember, it is still part of an examination submission, and it may be wise not to drop your guard completely.

Any parts of the acknowledgements that relate to the research itself – for example, libraries or experts consulted – should reinforce the strengths in your research. Avoid anything that hints at any sort of weakness or unguarded unorthodoxy that might alert the examiner to some deep fault-line in your research which might otherwise have gone unnoticed.

Similarly, it may be best to avoid saying anything too flippant, sentimental, stealthily self-aggrandising or exaggeratedly self-deprecating. Think how damning this might look if it turned out to be the prelude to a failed thesis.

Be considerate when addressing your supervisors: what you say here may be the first and last recorded opinion of them. Be careful that some hasty remark doesn't undo years of trust and respect.

As ever, a good guide is to look at previous theses, to get a feel for reading 'cold' someone else's idea of a measured personal tribute.

If all this needs several drafts to get it shipshape and politically correct, you may feel as if the acknowledgements constitute the single most thoroughly prepared page in the whole thesis. But remember, of all your thesis, the acknowledgements page is likely to be the page most thoroughly read, by the greatest number of people. Not only is it the juiciest page in the thesis, but possibly the only one anyone will understand.

The late submission fee

The only fixed dates in the PhD calendar are ignominious ones:

- the date your money runs out (if you had any in the first place);

- the date beyond which you have to pay a late submission fee for the privilege of submitting (if you ever get round to submitting); and

- the date after which you may be technically barred from ever submitting.

The prospect of any of those dates looming into view may be enough to send you over the edge.

You may think yourself entitled to feel that, whatever else, your thesis can never really be *late*, as long as it actually gets finished. After all, you are supposed to be doing timely, cutting-edge research, that has to be up-to date in order to pass. You may feel that your thesis is ahead of its time, and the only way in which you would be 'late' is if you died before you finished.

However, the bureaucracy do not see it that way: once a certain digit has clicked past, your research, no matter how earth-shattering, will be forever filed as 'late', only to be handled on payment of a suitable fee. This may seem extortionate; the university could charge as much as it likes, now that you have an examinable thesis.

But think of the costs if, to avoid being late, you were to submit prematurely. The cost of resubmission or outright failure would be high, if only financially. Risking incurring the late submission fee may be worth it to buy the time to give you the best possible chance of clearing it in one go.

Final printing

Printing deserves a section to itself, so here it is. You have consulted all the rules for how to lay out the title page, abstract and so on, and how to deal with bibliography and supplementary material, such as maps or videos. Reference to an existing successful thesis or two is – as ever – invaluable, in checking for how formats appear, how different alternative treatments are possible. Even if you intend to depart from the norm, knowing what the norm *is* is usually valuable.

Allow plenty of time for producing the final product. Printing out can be stressful, especially if you are using big files and complex diagrams that refuse to print correctly, are too big to squeeze through your printer buffer, or if the printer habitually seems to crash your computer.

One pitfall that could arise is if you attempt to print out on a computer you don't normally use. You may find that the word-processing programme may be set up somehow in a different format, and it could be that all the pagebreaks are in the wrong place, or greyscale comes out as a poor black and white stipple. You then have to reformat the thesis, or at least certain crucial pages. It helps, then, if you can plan to format the thesis on the computer printer you intend to produce the final version on – or harmonise settings in advance to avoid unexpected hiccups in the final stages.

The stress of all these practically-inclined tasks is magnified if you are trying to do them in a hurry. Like all other parts of the PhD process, it is still likely to take longer than you thought – simply printing off that many pages can take hours, even without mishaps. Have faith in Murphy's Law: anything that can go wrong will, sooner or later. Like pages jamming and inks or toner running out mid-print, or pages unaccountably being printed squint – and you didn't notice and went away and came back a hundred pages later to find the whole festering pile is useless.

To minimise stress, you may benefit from getting out of other people's hair. You might consider doing the final production and printing where and when you can be alone, for example, at home, or out of hours – perhaps even overnight. You can concentrate on the final thesis 100%, and keep your final hurrahs or curses to yourself. On the other hand, running out of ink or paper at midnight could be hair-tearingly frustrating, so be prepared and stock up in advance. Whichever way you approach it, leave yourself enough time, because if you are too tired you may just end up making mistakes, and have to reprint everything again (this is a hint that sometimes it could be more productive to leave something unfinished overnight and go home to bed!).

And on the final-final print run, be especially careful to look out for errors in the early pages as, if some last minute change has to be added in towards the beginning, it could mean reprinting almost the whole document.

Having said all that, it must be one of the most satisfying experiences of all those years of work, watching the final pages coming off the printer, knowing that all going well, it should be for the last ever time.

Theses!

For so long 'the thesis' has been an eternally pending, looming 'thing'. Now, you have printed it out, and suddenly not one but several have materialised. No sooner have you 'the thesis', but you are now staggering around with several huge *theses* for all the world to see.

The person whose dinner guest spilled wine over the final printed version of the thesis

Yes, really; and it was spilled over all three copies of the thesis. As a student, you will probably not be living in a large house or flat, and if you have visitors round for a drink, it is not beyond the realms of possibility that someone will spill a drink.

This is precisely what happened to our unfortunate friend, when said guest placed their glass of wine awkwardly on a side table on which the print-outs sat, and as a consequence spilled the entire glassful over the three final copies of the thesis.

Result: one cheerfully apologetic guest who didn't grasp the full import of what they had done, and one quietly apoplectic PhD student who said not to worry, it wasn't a problem. And technically, that was true, but the thesis did have to be printed out all over again, which is no joke at this stage.

So the message is simple. Be *absolutely, totally, completely paranoid* about protecting the print-out of your thesis. Keep it somewhere warm and dry and flat, and don't let anything or anyone near it (including pets). Because if printing out your thesis the first time is depressing and frustrating, having to print it out again, in its entirety, as a result of a silly, avoidable accident, is plain anger-inducing. It's as simple as that.

Finishing

When is your thesis finished? When it is submitted for examination? Or when you have defended it at the viva? Or when it is finally ensconced in your university library, after all possible correction has been done forever? Obviously, the last of these chronologically is the final and ultimate completion. However, the most emotional feeling of completion may come when you have printed your last page and dispatched it to the binders. That is when you may have the strongest feeling of a point of closure, a point of no return. At that point, in effect, it has mortally passed on, although it may later have some remedial treatment before final interment.

You are likely to feel any or all of: relief, euphoria, disbelief, climax, anticlimax, quiet satisfaction, unbounded joy, numbness. Perhaps any sense of sheer outrageous glee and shouting to the world that you have finished is tempered by the fact that you are worried about riling those who never wanted or never got a PhD themselves.

You may feel disorientated, especially if you had been in an oppressive, obsessive regime of thesis-production, with every waking hour thinking of it, and if you have no immediately competing occupation afterwards. Although you have been looking forward to this for so long, it is hard immediately to disengage, and get used to life without it.

You may even feel a sense of denial – being unable to come to terms with the fact that the thesis is no longer 'there'. After months and years, it has been a dominating concern, always staring you in the face, forever hanging over you, lurking in the background, or disconcertingly hovering out of the corner of your eye, patiently waiting for an unguarded moment to say 'excuse me, but...' So it can come as a strange new experience that it is no longer there, and there is absolutely nothing more to be done.

Now you see it!

A remarkable transformation can take place once your thesis – the invisible intellectual feat you have been grappling with all those years – finally becomes a finished, tangible product. Your thesis, which to other people has so often been an object of incomprehension, derision and hopelessness, has now become a sight to behold: the sheer size and weight of it, the gold letters on the binding. Ironically, what had been an abstract cerebral challenge is now acclaimed in all its crude physical glory, as a gleaming, thumping great doorstop!

11
Examination

When the viva voce looms, it is wise to remember that you have already done the hard part: choosing your topic, writing the thesis and choosing the examiner. So get those bits right and you should not have to worry too much about the viva. That said, the prospect of having to defend your thesis remains an unpleasant one, and this chapter is based on an old counsel of war: know your enemy (or examiner).

Outcomes of the viva voce

These are the possible outcomes of a viva:

1. Outright failure (rare in the extreme; usually a consequence of the student ignoring the supervisor's advice).

2. The offer of an MPhil (very rare; same reasons as above).

3. A requirement to re-enter the exam with a substantially revised thesis (unusual, and could be considered a 'pass with major corrections'; usually means that you cannot make the required corrections within three months – a second viva is possible, but not mandatory).

4. Pass with minor corrections (by far the most common outcome – corrections to be made within three months, typically).

5. Pass with no corrections (unusual, and great if you get it).

You can reasonably expect that if your supervisor has let you submit your thesis, you will pass. If you get nice examiners, they may not require any corrections (assuming no typographic errors and so forth). More likely, you will have to add a couple of references, change a chart and clarify one or two points. Once you have got this far, you are all but home and dry (see also Choosing your examiners, below; Making corrections after the viva, in Chapter 12).

Choosing your examiners

Formally, your supervisor or university examination board may be responsible for appointing your examiners. But typically you will be offered the chance to suggest the choice of appointees yourself – not least because you should be best placed to know the experts in the field.

You might spend on average half a year per chapter, but only half a day choosing your examiners. Yet the particular choice of examiner could have as much influence on the outcome of your examination as your methodological framework you laboured for half a year to achieve. So you should choose your examiners with due care.

You can reasonably think of your examiners as your audience, or readership, albeit a well-informed one. It will pay, then, to target your product to what an interested person in your field needs to know, and to your examiners' likely boredom threshold. And of course they will know much less about your topic than you do – remember that you are the expert here – so while you should be careful to tell them what they need to know, there is no point in labouring away on parts of the thesis that your examiners will not understand, or filling out elaborate appendices that your examiners will not read.

You should also be aware of your examiner's pet references (often their own), and time spent on the internet finding out about their broader research interests that might not be obvious from their publications can pay dividends. Equally, you can learn what they *won't* understand in your thesis, and write it accordingly.

Besides the academic considerations, there are also personal ones. Do the examiners get on well with your supervisor? Are you challenging their theories (and therefore challenging their egos)? Younger or less experienced examiners have a reputation for being tougher than their older, more experienced counterparts, who intuitively know a PhD when they see one.

Finally, you will be choosing your examiners in conjunction with your supervisor, who will have their own ideas of who would be appropriate. You might find that you disagree on who would be suitable, and then it becomes a matter of negotiation (though ultimately the choice may be out of your hands). And that, you doubtless realise, is yet another reason for trying to develop a good working relationship with your supervisor. So choose carefully (see also Your relationship with your supervisor, in Chapter 3).

About the examiner

As a PhD candidate, your viva may seem like your impending nemesis, and your examiner the judge, jury and executioner. But to the examiner, the viva is only one part of a wider pursuit. To your examiner, the examination of a PhD thesis could be any or all of the following.

■ A gratefully accepted mark of status in being invited to examine at your institution in the first place: something to put on their CV.

■ A chance to network, not least with your supervisors and any other examiners: a chance to be seen to be 'on the scene'.

■ Possibly a pleasant break from daily routine, in visiting your city – as one might regard a jaunt (albeit a 'work trip') to a meeting or conference.

■ A useful exercise in 'intelligence' in learning what other PhD theses are like, which may enrich their own capability as a supervisor who has to get their PhD students to pass a similar test.

■ Just possibly, the chance to gain some insights into cutting edge work (i.e. yours!), or access to an expanded set of references, or, at the very least, if your thesis contains nothing much useful, that they are confirmed in their belief they are unassailable in their own mastery of the topic.

As well as indicating that examiners are, after all, humans too, any or all of these could mean that the examiner is already predisposed to feeling the thesis examination is a worthy academic exercise they are engaged in, quite apart from what goes on during the viva itself. Bearing this point of view in mind won't rescue a flawed thesis, but it may help a candidate feel less unnecessarily anxious about defending a sound one.

Averting corrections

Clearly it is better to avert the possibility of having to do corrections, rather than wait until your examiner points them out. Avoiding corrections is not only a boost to the esteem but saves the effort and expense of reprinting and rebinding the thesis.

Here is a list of common things needing correction, and suggested ways of averting them.

1. Errata and errors of clarity

These mistakes are obvious to almost any reader. For example, spelling mistakes, diagrams inserted upside down, wrong captions or missing references. These are things that a primary school kid could spot. Then, there are things like lack of clarity of argument, or downright bad English, which should be clear enough to any adult reader. All of these kinds of flaws are very visible and are likely to be picked up and require correction. For example, it is much easier to spot something you put in that's wrong, than something you left out that should have been in. The examiner would hardly be doing their job if they failed to point them out.

Suggested ways of averting the problem:

(a) Invite someone non-technical to read your thesis – for example, a partner or family member. They should be able to spot basic mistakes, or find fault in your writing style, as they will not be worrying about your impenetrable technical arguments.

(b) Invite someone to specifically check for the 'mechanical' parts – could be another PhD candidate at your stage, for whom you could return the favour.

(c) Invite a knowledgeable person – such as a professional in industry, or senior undergraduate – to read the whole thing, perhaps for a fee. They should be competent and interested enough to spot problems with your arguments, without their being a rival (as a junior PhD in the same field might be perceived). Unlike your long-suffering supervisor or friends, the thesis should be completely fresh to them, and perhaps even educational.

(d) Use a spell-checker. Also, double-check numbers – eg captions, footnote order, dates, years, etc.

(e) If at any stage you are grappling with some problematic diagram or table or reference, consider the effect of leaving it out, which may do less damage than leaving it in wrong.

2. Examiner wants more or different material included

The examiner cannot find fault with what you have written as such, but feels that you could have given more attention to other areas, or that your whole thesis would be better directed to some other point of focus. This could especially arise if the topic is tangential to the examiner's own specialist area, and they would find it more 'balanced' if it included more of their worldview in it. In the most extreme cases, the examiner is trying to criticise the 'wrong thesis' (i.e. a hypothetical thesis that is not the one they have before them).

Suggested ways of averting the problem:

(a) Choose your examiner carefully.

(b) Be sure to flag up carefully at the outset of the thesis what the scope and approach taken is, in order that there is no danger of confusion with some other (unwritten) thesis.

Suggested ways of dealing with it if it arises:

(a) Use the viva to (i) make clear that the thesis they are criticising is not the one you submitted for examination; (ii) put up a robust defence of why you did not do 'the other thesis'. In other words, convince the examiner that what you did is complete and consistent in itself.

(b) It may be necessary to bow gracefully to your examiner's wishes and add in some extra material which adds to (and in your examiner's opinion, completes) treatment of the topic. At least, what they want added should hopefully be (i) clearly specified by the examiner and (ii) not conflict with what is already there. If not, a more robust defence before acceding may be necessary.

3. Interfering philosophies

It could be that your scope is similar to your examiner's but the detailed approach is different or conflicting. Here the problem is that no matter how well you did your research, the examiner will only grudgingly acknowledge its merit, or not give it merit at all. This could happen where your topic and your examiner's specialism are close enough to interfere with each other, but not so close as to be compatible. Another way it could arise is where applying an approach from one discipline to a new discipline – especially if the examiner is not sympathetic with the field from which you are applying your method. This is potentially one of the most damaging situations to find oneself in, since it could imply a good piece of work having to be rewritten to fit the examiner's point of view, perhaps in a way that makes the end product less coherent overall.

Suggested ways of averting the problem:

(a) Choose your examiner carefully, to avoid interfering philosophies.

(b) Work out your topic carefully with your supervisor in the first place, if there is any doubt that the application of method from field A will ruffle feathers in field B.

4. Thesis too shallow or overblown

In this scenario, the examiner is a real expert and authority in your topic, and simply finds that your work is incomplete or unoriginal, or overblown in its claims. Here, the examiner is the best person to judge your thesis, but finds it wanting. They are well placed not only to find fault but also to give good advice on what needs correction. So look on the bright side: your thesis (and learning) should at least be improved by the corrective experience.

A way to think of this is to imagine that you yourself are examining an undergraduate or Master's dissertation (perhaps your own) on the topic of your PhD, where the shorter work might easily seem shallow, patchy or corny in comparison with your understanding of the topic. What would be forgiveable is if the treatment at least meets its own objectives in its own terms (e.g. an overview of a topic, or a limited analysis of a particular part of the topic). What is less forgiveable is if it appears to be simply rehashing existing work, or claiming to be the definitive work on a topic when it isn't, while missing out or dismissing prematurely the work of others.

Suggested ways of averting the problem:

(a) Make sure arguments are robust, and scope of claimed mastery clearly delimited.

(b) Be familiar with the field of expertise of your examiner, and make judicious citations to their work or their own 'pet references' where appropriate (but don't overdo it!).

5. Flawed thesis

Here, the thesis is not up to PhD standard; the method is faulty, or the analysis is unsatisfactory. This is the point which is most connected with the role of your supervisor. Your supervisor is basically employed to ensure the thesis does not go wrong for one of these reasons. Avoid it by having a good supervisor, and by submitting your thesis when your supervisor has indicated it is 'examinable'.

Preparing for the exam

'I know this made sense when I wrote it, but now... well I just don't understand it' is a common complaint of PhD students returning to their thesis in the run-up to the viva. The month or two (or more) since they handed it in have passed, and now the viva voce looms. So how should you prepare for this momentous (and, possibly frightening) occasion?

First, read your thesis; while some bits might make you groan inwardly, there will be plenty of other bits that give you a pleasant surprise, an 'Oh, it's not that bad actually' moment. Remember that your supervisor would not have let you submit it in the first place if they had not believed it 'examinable'. What you now need to do is make sure that you are familiar with it, so that you can quickly flip to the relevant page in the viva when one of the examiners asks you the inevitable question on something that's already covered.

You may wish to make a running summary of the contents of each chapter, if only to prevent your mind from switching as you graze over the familiar arguments. It forces you to pay attention, and weigh up the significance of each passage, and its contribution to the whole.

You should look for weaknesses, as the examiners will, and think of ways that you would address them were you to do the research again; after all, one of the requirements of a PhD is that you should be able to offer a dispassionate critique of your own work. Bear in mind too that a PhD is a limited piece of work, so it is not unreasonable to think of ways in which, given greater resources, you could have improved upon it. Perhaps, if time and money had permitted, you would have gathered more data, whether by visiting more obscure archives, interviewing more people, or using more sophisticated instrumentation. Or you might have indulged in much more sophisticated analysis of your data had your funding not run out – assuming you had any in the first place. If you have done the PhD part-time, you might want to reflect on how doing it full-time might have changed your approach by enabling the exploration of more speculative research avenues. Of course some of this you will have covered in the section on areas of further research; some you will not.

Doubtless you will spot other minor errors – typing mistakes and so forth: be aware of them, but no more. If the examiners pick them up, fine; if not, consider yourself lucky. You won't have a problem spotting your errors, but you should also look for more positive things too. In particular, you should be conscious of the value of your work – the so-called 'original contribution', and of any practical or policy implications that might flow from your work.

One way of smoothing this process is to have a 'mock viva', in which your supervisors or others make a trial run of your examination. Although it can never be the same as the real thing, this may help get you used to verbal expression and justification of your arguments. Most basically, it can prepare you for the experience of having to sit down and have other people, armed with your thesis, fire questions at you, and the state of being on the defensive for a sustained period. It may also open up new perspectives on your work.

Defending your thesis

When it comes down to it, the examination is a defence of your thesis. In other words, it is the thesis that is on trial, not you. So, for your own peace of mind, you have to think of yourself as the smart attorney – it is your thesis that is the 'accused'. You know better than anyone else its strengths and weaknesses, and have prepared a case on its behalf. Sure, you are sympathetic to it; you're on its side. But you also have to consider your own position in front of your professional peers. You cannot afford to be damned along with the accused. If the accused proves wanting under scrutiny, you would do your professional reputation no harm to admit the fault and try to minimise the sentence.

Minimising the sentence is indeed what you are trying to do – the 'sentence' being the amount of rewriting to do afterwards.

The viva is not an 'oral exam' – it is not a test of your verbal eloquence or the brilliance of your arguments. Your job is to get the thesis acquitted – not to show off your years of learning and erudition. The thesis will stand or fall by its own testimony. There is more than enough written in the thesis to incriminate itself. There is also more than enough in there to get away with it. Your job is to point to the evidence – the arguments already in there.

If the examiners appear to ask a 'too obvious' question, don't be fooled into trying to invent a novel answer. The question only seems obvious to you – and the obvious answer not novel – because you have spent the last half dozen years writing the darned thing. Recall, they read the last two chapters on the train yesterday, two weeks after they first read the introduction. So, the chances are they missed something in the text, rather than you missing something out.

If your thesis is well written and your examiners are well chosen, then it is more likely that your thesis will be read with the care it deserves in the first place. If your thesis is too boring or badly written, your examiners may not have had the time or inclination to understand it properly. Remember, they may just be bluffing their way through being examiners. In this case, they may be slightly anxious that they themselves are not shown up in front of you, or each other, by missing some fiendishly abstruse or glaringly obvious point. This is bad news, because if they are feeling insecure, they may try to get their retaliation in first.

So, you want to avoid anything too adversarial, or clever-clever. Just like writing the thesis itself, your aim in the examination is to lead your examiners painlessly through understanding in a diligent, helpful and user-friendly way. All being well, they will have read the thesis, understood it, and be sufficiently satisfied to acquit it.

Rehearsing your defence

The PhD is in some senses an intellectual marathon where you are just about the only person to cover the ground all the way. You may be forced to keep your own intellectual company over a long distance, and you may not truly know what impact your thesis has until the examination, or some time after.

In fact, there is a danger that the examination is one of the few chances you really get to chew over the ideas in the thesis seriously with another person. Your friends and colleagues – even your supervisor – will have read bits and pieces, perhaps several times over – but not fresh in a single stream of argument, demanding an immediate mental grasp from end to end.

So, after years of grappling with that-which-cannot-be-talked-about – years of seeing people's eyes glaze over as you mention generalised-cost-minimising-algorithms or dissecting amphibians' kidneys – it could be a dangerous burst of attention when two experts in your field suddenly turn up on your doorstep and ask provocative, stimulating and informed questions about your thesis.

The chances are, they will ask something that sparks off something new in your mind. The temptation will be to pick up the thought and run with it – into dangerous new territory, where you may soon find yourself lost, without support, and at the mercy of your examiners. Instead, you would be well advised to stick to the thesis – after all, you have spent years slaving over every carefully rehearsed argument, caveat and footnote to get the facts, inferences and speculations in just the right balance. There is no point in throwing this all away by being sidetracked into a hypothetical argument about extraterrestrial biochemistry.

So it can be handy to get all your arguments aired in advance. It can be helpful to talk through the various ideas in the thesis – probably a variety of ideas with a variety of people – and make sure any brainstorming hits you before the examination.

Even if you had a genuine eureka moment in the exam, what would be the result? You would be admitting to something you hadn't thought of before. Your examiners would surely be pleased they had teased out this nugget – and they would just as surely ask you to put it into the thesis. Result: an own goal, and a long sentence of painful remedial surgery.

The day of the viva

The day of the viva, if at all possible, should be given over entirely to the PhD. You may have a job by the time your viva comes round, so take the day off if you can, and give yourself plenty of time to get ready for it, and get to the exam. Your basic aim here is to be relaxed or at least to be concerned only with the matter in hand – the PhD.

Going into your examination may feel like going into an inter-view – you have on your smartest clothes, carefully chosen tie or killer shoes. It may have the feeling of foreboding of a seri-ous business that not only your future hangs on, but represents the culmination of the investment of years, rather than the couple of days it took you to dust off your CV and prepare for a job interview.

But a big difference between an interview and the PhD examina-tion is that the examination is really about you and your thesis. Whereas, at the end of the day, a job interview is really all about the job, and how you might fit into it.

In a job interview, you could be asked almost any question about your carefully spun past or your recklessly promised future. But in your PhD exam, the whole thing revolves around your work. Questions will be asked on your thesis. In this sense, you are in control. Or at least, you have had the main influence on shaping the agenda for the examination conversation.

And, unlike a job interview, you are not trying to second guess the needs of your interrogators, or make yourself out as something you are not. And you are not competing with some phantom alternative candidates for what is your prize.

You have done the hard part – writing the thesis. It is up to the examiners to get their heads round your thesis, and your duty to assist them.

Heisenberg's viva

It may come as a small reassurance that even future Nobel Laureates have had their PhD problems. Physicist Werner Heisenberg (he of the Uncertainty Principle) received a vicious mauling at the hands of one of his examiners during his viva voce. For although a brilliant theorist, Heisenberg's practical inclinations fell sharply below the level that one examiner felt appropriate. Disdain proved inadequate to the said examiner, who felt obliged to resort to complete outrage at the fact that this young 22-year-old candidate professed not to know how to wire up a simple electrical circuit, and shouted that Heisenberg should most certainly not be granted his doctorate. Fortunately, Heisenberg's advisor ensured that common sense prevailed, and his other examiners, recognising the young genius for what he was, gave him his PhD. He was awarded the Nobel physics prize nine years later.

12
The Afterlife

The viva is over, and the verdict delivered. For the first time in years you should have a definite grasp of what you have to do to finish, and your mind can turn to 'life after thesis'.

Making corrections after the viva

Not everyone has to make corrections after the oral exam, but most do. This section is intended for that unfortunate majority. We won't dwell too much here on this particularly unpleasant phase of the process, but just offer a few helpful pointers. The most important point to remember is that if you are now working, your PhD work rate will plummet, probably to well under half of what it was when you were studying, no matter how diligent you intend to be.

This is not because of lack of time, though, because there are still plenty of evenings and weekends in which to do the work. It has more to do with the fact that the PhD quickly becomes rather remote, not least because, having moved on yourself, you want to leave it behind. Add to this the fact that your new job will take most of your energy. Finally, throw in the fact that making what may well feel like trivial, pointless, misinformed and irrelevant corrections (even if they actually are not) at the behest of examiners is just plain tedious at best, and at worst can make you feel genuinely angry and depressed, and you have a recipe for reluctance that only you can overcome.

So the best advice we can offer is this: do exactly what the examiners want you to do, as soon as you can, and just get it out of the way. There is absolutely no way in which you can make this part of the PhD pleasant. The worst is over, so just finish the job and hand it in. If you have to pay a fee for re-entering the exam – a possibility if you have anything more than 'minor corrections' – bite the bullet and pay up. Then you can put the whole thing behind you, and wait for the certificate to plop onto your doormat. Then you are a doctor.

Graduation

Unlike when you graduate from your first degree, which is usually a big communal celebration, with all your classmates in tow, when you are awarded your doctorate you may not know anyone else there, and it may therefore feel like something of an anti-climax.

Although to you the viva was the big day, for your family your graduation marks the completion of your PhD. Besides, they can at least tell their friends that their son/daughter now *really* has a PhD, and is no longer 'a student' doing something they can't explain. Finally, there are precious few occasions when you can celebrate definite accomplishments during your doctoral study. It is, after all, the final chance for a celebration, so if you are of a mind to enjoy the moment to the full, go right ahead: you deserve it!

Isaac Asimov

Isaac Asimov was one of the best-known and most prolific writers in science and science fiction. He is accredited with over 500 books published over a range of topics including science, technology, literature, arts, languages and religion.

He managed to combine his breadth of interests with the specialised discipline of academia – up to a point. Following Bachelor's and Master's degrees, he gained a Doctorate in Chemistry from Columbia University in 1948. He subsequently went on to become an Associate Professor in Biochemistry, although ceased this occupation (in all but title) in order to concentrate on writing – rather than being a 'mediocre researcher'. He eventually was awarded a full professorship in 1979.

Asimov's doctoral study was interrupted by four years' wartime service. During his period of doctoral study he also completed two of the *Foundation* trilogy, which won a Hugo Prize. On passing his PhD viva he is said to have got drunk on Manhattans in celebration, and spent the night giggling and repeating '*Doctor* Asimov'.

Building on your doctoral research

Your doctoral research could become the foundation for an academic career – or at least, an entrée to your first post-doctoral research job. If you framed your own PhD topic, you effectively wrote your own job description, lasting a number of years. However, this opportunity to set your own agenda is not so straightforward in the immediate post-doctoral years.

Post-doctoral research

Perhaps the most common way of gaining research experience is via a post-doctoral research job. These appointments are usually set up as part of a specific project, and run for a fixed term. If your doctoral topic is part of a recognised programme of research, it may be that there are plentiful opportunities to be employed more or less closely in the area of your PhD topic. If, however, your research interests are more specialised, or fiscally unfashionable, you may have to work to a different research agenda in the first instance.

A variety of research fellowships exist which are set up specifically to encourage the researcher to become established in their academic field, geared to providing the requisite combination of research experience and publication, rather than simply being someone else's research assistant. These fellowships tend to be competitive; check eligibility carefully, and try to find out the likely ratio of applicants to awards. Some awards require a demonstrable research track record; others are intended for 'young researchers', or those who have just completed a thesis – beware of falling in between two stools here.

Academic Research

Your main aim may be to become an established academic, such as a lecturer, or ultimately, a professor. Such a position is likely to involve a mixture of research and teaching. The PhD qualification has traditionally been seen as a qualification to teach, although, of course, a PhD itself does not require any teaching skill or experience. In any case, to be in a competitive position for landing such an academic post, a track record in research may be decisive.

Becoming an established academic allows you a certain amount of time and freedom to pursue your own research agenda. By the time you reach this stage, your PhD thesis or topic may be a distant memory, but the PhD qualification itself will always be underpinning your career.

The prospects for a career solely in academic research are limited, because there are fewer pure research (non-teaching) jobs available on a permanent basis. Moreover, some institutions specifically disallow those not already in an academic position to hold a research grant – or disallow grant-holders to draw their own salary from it. Ironically, a PhD graduate may first have to find a teaching position, in order to be allowed to direct their own research.

There are also opportunities for research outside academia, in independent institutes, working for government and industry. Wherever you end up, you may thrive in your chosen career, but the research may never be quite as intensive and personal as the good old days as a PhD student.

Turning your thesis into a book

There are at least three clear reasons for writing an academic book. Firstly, it is a record and repository of your research, and an exposition of your scholarship. So producing a book can look good on your CV, even if no one buys it. Secondly, it might make some money. Not necessarily the value of labour you put into it; but a book that makes some profit will look good to your publisher, even if no one reads it. Thirdly, if people actually read the book, it might have some influence. You could meet any of these three objectives without writing a book; but if these are your objectives, writing a book could achieve all three in one go.

If you can write a PhD thesis, you should have the ability, self-confidence and persistence to get a book published – though not necessarily on your exact topic. An abstruse topic only understood by you, your supervisor and your examiners will have less of a market than a more general topic on some big issue of the day. What makes a good thesis topic does not necessarily make a good book topic – and vice versa. But if your thesis topic equates with the book you always wanted to write, then it's possible that doing a doctorate, if not the most direct route, could be an instrumental stepping stone.

Turning a thesis into a book can be particularly satisfying, as the main slog of the research has been done, and the burden of 'finishing the doctorate' lifted. In fact – and this is why we mention it at all – even just thinking about turning the thesis into a book can be helpful for your PhD. For a start, it encourages you to think of your audience, and be a spur to clear writing, since this will save rewriting later. You can regard the proposed book as a repository of all the more speculative or ill-fitting parts of your work, and so curb the inclination to squeeze too much into the thesis, or to veer into too many dangerous byways, with the threat of vulture-examiners circling overhead.

The very idea of the book can help keep thesis completion in perspective as an unremarkable finite task. The burden of the immortal magnum opus then transfers to 'the book to come'…

Top tips on doing a PhD

1. Be clear of your objectives and reasons for wanting to do a PhD, as these will influence decisions on your progress and ultimate completion of your doctorate. Also be aware that your supervisors and funders may have slightly different objectives, which might diverge as time goes on.

2. Get to know other PhD students (and successful ex-PhD students), and learn from how they coped.

3. Understand that doing a PhD is neither quite like the academic challenges you have been successful in up until now, nor quite like the kind of job you are likely to be doing afterwards.

4. Although a PhD may be an ultimate, 'pure', personal academic attainment, it is part of a wider human system in which you may have to lean on other people or play politics from time to time.

5. Know the rules; submitting the wrong form, or submitting a thesis in the wrong format, or having the 'wrong' supervisor or examiner could cost months of effort.

6. Doing a PhD may be more like a war of attrition than a single heroic assault; knowledge of the territory and tenacity may be just as important qualities as strategy or intellectual firepower.

7. Judge your progress by a variety of criteria, not just the apparent progress of other people on other research trajectories or other careers.

8. Get a range of advice from different quarters; there is no single 'best way' to do any PhD.

9. Although you may sometimes feel you are taking up your institution's space and your supervisor's time, you are also a positive statistic in their accounts. You are a client, not a parasite.

10. Doing a PhD may be the most challenging thing you ever do, intellectually; but therein lies its capacity to be the most stimulating and rewarding experience, from which the rest of your career can always draw strength and inspiration.

Useful Websites

National Postgraduate Committee

An organisation set up specifically to address the concerns of postgraduates:

> The National Postgraduate Committee is the representative body for postgraduates in the UK. We are made up of student representatives from educational institutions with postgraduate students. The NPC aims to promote the interests of postgraduates studying in the UK, while remaining politically non-aligned. The Committee holds an annual conference, and publishes various guidelines and codes of practice.

> The NPC aims to provide value-added services to our affiliated institutions. Wherever on this site you see this symbol, it is to indicate that a site resource is available only to connections from an affiliated institution's network, or to individuals connecting from home with a username and password.

From their website

www.npc.org.uk

The UK Research Councils

The primary funders of PhD research in the United Kingdom.

Websites

The Research Councils UK (a gateway to all the research councils) **www.research-councils.ac.uk**

Biotechnology and Biological Sciences Research Council (BBSRC)
www.bbsrc.ac.uk

Economic and Social Research Council (ESRC)
www.esrc.ac.uk

Engineering and Physical Sciences Research Council (EPSRC)
www.epsrc.ac.uk

Medical Research Council (MRC)
www.mrc.ac.uk

Natural Environment Research Council (NERC)
www.nerc.ac.uk

Particle Physics and Astronomy Research Council (PPARC)
www.pparc.ac.uk

Arts and Humanities Research Board (AHRB)
www.ahrb.ac.uk

Further reading

Doing Postgraduate Research, S. Potter, SAGE Publications.

A Handbook for Writers of English: Punctuation, common practice and usage, J.G.Taylor, How To Books.

How to Get a PhD: A handbook for students and their supervisors, E. Phillips and D. Pugh, Open University Press.

How to Write a Thesis, R. Murray, Open University Press.

Practical Research Methods: A user-friendly guide to mastering research techniques and projects, C. Dawson, How To Books.

Student Survival Guide: What to expect and how to handle it – insider advice on university life, L. Clarke and J. Hawkins, How To Books.

Surviving Your Dissertation: A comprehensive guide to content and process, K. Rudestam & R. Newton, SAGE Publications.

Writing Your Dissertation: How to plan, prepare and present successful work, D. Swetnan, How To Books.

Index

entries in **bold** refer to sections dealing specifically with the topic.

How To Books are available through all good bookshops, or you can order direct from us through Grantham Book Services.

Tel: +44 (0)1476 541080
Fax: +44 (0)1476 541061
Email: orders@gbs.tbs-ltd.co.uk

Or via our website

www.howtobooks.co.uk

To order via any of these methods please quote the title(s) of the book(s) and your credit card number together with its expiry date.

For further information about our books and catalogue, please contact:

How To Books
3 Newtec Place
Magdalen Road
Oxford OX4 1RE

Visit our web site at

www.howtobooks.co.uk

Or you can contact us by email at
info@howtobooks.co.uk

If you want to know how ... to conduct effective research

"I've broken away from the traditional academic social research book, and tried to present something which is more user-friendly and people-orientated. I've tried to put across complicated issues in a way that can be understood by anyone who's interested in their topic." – *Dr Catherine Dawson*

Practical Research Methods
A user-friendly guide to mastering research techniques and projects.
Dr Catherine Dawson

"All students should read this book. I now understand what research is all about – I've even got my head around the theory as well as the actual methods. I've completed the research for my dissertation and it was much easier than I thought, thanks to this book." – *Amazon Reader Review*

ISBN 1 85703 829 0

If you want to know how ... to write an essay

"This book will be of benefit to students at any age from 14 to MA level. I believe that those students who begin to use it at 14 will still be benefiting from it in any tertiary courses they take up. I have outlined the principles and shown them in action in as simple and direct a manner as possible. The essential advice doesn't change from one level to the other: the quality and depth of the essay required at different stages will be forthcoming if the skills have been developed and the knowledge obtained."
– *Brendan Hennessy*

Writing an Essay
Simple techniques to transform your course work and examinations
Brendan Hennessy

This lively, practical guide takes you through the whole process. With it you'll write essays of distinction every time.

"There's a lot of good sense in this book." – *Times Educational Supplement*

"If you're a student buy it." – *Writer's Monthly*

1 85703 846 0

If you want to know how ... to write your dissertation

"This book is based on the real experiences of students who need ideas for planning and producing a good piece of work without the stress and total disruption of their personal life. Mature students especially will enjoy the pragmatic approach which still makes no concessions to the quality and integrity of the final product." – *Derek Swetnam*

Writing Your Dissertation
The bestselling guide to planning, preparing and presenting first-class work
Derek Swetnam

"I wish I had read this book before I had started to write my dissertation. The chapters are relevant and helpful and contain information such as some of the most common spelling mistakes. This book is a great basic start." – *Amazon Reader Review*

"This book has been a lifesaver! Half way through a dissertation I suddenly realised that I was drifting aimlessly. This book gave me guidance and helped me to structure my dissertation plan when I needed it most. I would definitely recommend it to others!"– *Amazon Reader Review*

1 85703 662 X